A Heartfelt Undertaking

Rebecca Lyons

Publisher: Rebecca Lyons

Printer: Ingram Sparks

Editor: Sheelagh Wegman AE

Cover design: Cathy McAuliffe

Design and typeset: Beverly Waldie

This book is dedicated to my dad, Steven Lyons.
You fostered my love of reading as a child
and your belief in me never wavered.
I wish you had been here to see this finished.

Human bones part of a coat of arms on display in Sedlec Ossuary, a Roman Catholic Chapel found below the Cemetery Church of All Saints in Sedlec, Kutna Hora, Czech Republic

A report for the

WINSTON CHURCHILL MEMORIAL TRUST

To investigate the human relationship to death and ceremony through

alternative approaches and technologies

CONTENTS

Chandelier of human bones hanging in Sedlec Ossuary, a Roman Catholic Chapel found below the Cemetery Church of All Saints in Sedlec, Kutna Hora, Czech Republic

KEYWORDS

family-led funeral
death literacy
death and dying
end of life doula
home funeral guide
home death care
natural burial
alkaline hydrolysis
community capacity
compassionate communities
hospice
palliative care
contemporary funeral industry

ACKNOWLEDGMENTS

It is true what they say: it really does take a village to raise children, to care for the dying and to perform the kind of research and produce the kind of report that will hopefully make a valuable and meaningful impact on my fellow Australians and how we 'do' dying and death in this country.

First, I would like to sincerely acknowledge and thank the Churchill Trust for the opportunity to travel and learn from people worldwide. It has been an invaluable experience and the support and guidance I have received from them has been remarkable. The flexibility provided and the belief they have in the work of the Fellows is a very generous gift; it is an honour to have been the recipient of such an award and the faith and trust that accompanies it.

I would like to especially thank Dr Philip Thomson and Patricia Corby of the Tasmanian Churchill Trust whose interest and encouragement has meant so much to me.

To the delightful lady I am so pleased to call friend, Christine Howard; without you none of this would have been possible. You believed in me, introduced me

Left to Right: Dr Annetta Mallon, Dr Pia Interlandi, Claire Turnham and Rebecca Lyons at the 2019 National Home Funeral Alliance conference in Minnesota, USA

to what a Churchill Fellowship was and told me that I was not only capable of it but that I deserved it. I am forever grateful for you, your advice and guidance.

To the two beautiful women who believed in me and generously gave of themselves to put pen to paper to provide references for my Churchill application – Danielle Conlan from Kindred Life and Libby Maloney from Natural Grace – I hope my original report and now this book in some way honours the faith you have displayed both in me and in this project.

This work would not have happened without the generosity of all the people who agreed to meet with me and share so openly about their lives, work and experiences. Yours was not only an incredible gift of time but a gift of trust which still humbles me. Thank you to all those I interviewed and spent time with, for being so willing to help me bring your experiences and your knowledge to Australia. Any mistakes or discrepancies in this text are entirely my own.

It was the love and support of my family that enabled me to make manifest the courage and capability to take off for 10 weeks around the world on my own. You helped me to believe I was capable of trying to make a difference in this world.

My dear Joey, you will never know how much I look up to you and value your support – you are my number one inspiration and you consistently make me want to be a better person; you have been the greatest blessing the universe bestowed upon me and I am gratefully, always learning from you.

Edwin Quilliam, it has been your passion and drive as much as my own that has helped me keep the vision and you have supported this emotionally, financially and practically as only a good and kind man could – thank you for your love and care.

To Sue Lyons, Steve Lyons, Daniel Lyons, Tala Foley, Justina Lyons, Georgia Lyons, Helen Riley and Letitia Riley, your encouragement has helped beyond words, you helped nurture my ability to go confidently into the world – something so incredibly important and appreciated.

I have a wonderful group of friends, each of whom have a special place in my heart. Many of them have provided an ear when I have needed it, encouragement when my confidence waned, a hand to hold when I needed support and a constant unwavering belief in me and this Fellowship journey – Dr Pia Interlandi, Mea Souris, Danielle Stokes, Dimity Lee, Gael Fraser,

A Sarcophagus in Terme di Diocleziano, National Roman Museum. Rome, Italy

Jaymie Murphy, Dr Kerrie Noonan, Claire Turnham MBE, Zenith Virago, Dr Annetta Mallon, Alan Bitton, Geordie Smith, Regina Chan, Ai-Ming Wong, Kym Dalgenis, Lyn Redwig, Leigh Connell, Jordan Cripps, Lyndal Thorne, Nikolai Nilsson, Colleen Frost, Tracey Rusden, Kartika Franks, Doug O'Neil, Tara Kelly, Katy Cooper, Anna Ekhdal, Kaili Cen and Karina Skegg you are all shining examples of fierceness, compassion, endurance, tenacity and strength; each of you to me in your own unique way.

To Khylie Watson, you are there wherever I turn, you remain the calm when everything else is a storm.

A special mention needs to be made of another incredible human. Grant Blake, you are the best psychologist and support I could have ever hoped for to help me traverse this thing we call life. You help me heal and help me see. You help me to find the space and courage to believe in myself and expand my potential; working with you is a gift to the person I am becoming.

Finally, to all the trailblazers and tenacious individuals worldwide who have gone before me and led the way in clearing space for this kind of publication, ensuring that it has a place in the conversation and a seat at the table of the Australian community's reclaiming of the end of life, I sincerely honour you with the deepest gratitude.

There will always be a place for rebels, pioneers and those with the courage to break new ground.

MY BACKGROUND

Historically, in the theatre, the act of taking a bow at the end of a performance was to relinquish the role played. It is a simple gesture steeped in symbolism that many of us overlook and over time the meaning has become somewhat lost.

But when our time comes, how do we want to bow out of life? How do we get comfortable relinquishing that role? What are the conscious and unconscious choices that we make around dying and death and why...? What do they mean and how do they impact the living?

I entered the funeral industry in 2011, in an administrative role, although I was clear in my interview that if I was going to stay in any industry, I wanted to learn all about it. I went into a heavily male-dominated workplace as it was then, and far from finding that a problem, I relished the opportunity to learn all I could from the deeply respectful men who were my colleagues. It was the perfect opportunity to learn 'old school' and I have remained grateful for it.

Over the years my skill set grew and in addition to the administrative functions, I worked in funeral directing, doing pre-planning and organising pre-payment for people. I did off-site presentations, talking to people one-on-one and in groups. I worked in the mortuary, learned to process ashes, design the multimedia for services and booklets, provide catering...

Eventually I ended up looking after the logistics as well – the staff, vehicle and asset allocations, rostering etc. It was a broad scope in a tight framework.

In 2016 I was feeling more and more that I was not helping people the way I wanted to. I believed in the necessity of what we were providing but the grief and bereavement outcomes that I was seeing in the families were sorely lacking. Too many people were walking through the door at a loss as to what to do and with no idea about what was even possible. There was an astoundingly low level of death literacy in the community and it was having negative impacts on people financially and emotionally.

I felt that we needed to do better.

In August 2016 I co-founded a group called You n' Taboo, designed to be a safe space for people to gather, talk about dying, death and to learn from each

Bec with the lid of a homemade coffin, painted in blackboard paint

other. It was a successful beginning with about 19 people gathering for Dying to Know Day that year.

You n' Taboo continued with monthly meetings but we found that after a while, people were not returning. I recently learned that this is a similar phenomenon shown in research out of Glasgow University relating to death cafés – people go for the needs they have at the time but do not often become regulars. We did not know that at the time.

Eventually, we decided to take the conversation into the community by holding public events, attending festivals, fairs and shows. My partner built a coffin for people to lie in and contemplate their mortality and many Tasmanians have availed themselves of that opportunity since.

You n' Taboo has been engaging now for over five years with people from varying demographics, all around the end of life.

In May 2017 I became redundant from my role in the contemporary funeral industry. In June that year we went on a family holiday and we talked with a variety of funeral directors and owner/operators of natural burial sites. I had been looking into ways of doing death and ceremony differently for a while by then and the 'on the ground' learning was invaluable. It shaped and solidified my ideas on what would be possible in Australia. I returned full of ideas and out of work and so I had to rethink my direction.

I got a job somewhere completely different, which gave me the freedom to create something within the death care industry – a new space of my own. I stepped up into public education, speaking to public groups, clubs, medical staff in facilities, holding workshops and Q&A sessions. I trained as an end of life doula and I became a regulated business, meaning I have equal status to the other funeral homes in Tasmania to offer a full funeral service and be hands-on with the dead, with a difference. A grassroots-style, back to basics, family-led funeral service which works to empower families to be a part of the after-death process and experience the social, emotional and financial benefits that offers.

This is where I was when I applied for and was awarded my Churchill Fellowship.

I had been watching things happening all over the world that were changing the face of how we do dying, death and ceremony and I was keen to learn more. As with any social or grassroots-style movement, there needs to be transparency and support; there is little use in a whole bunch of people trying to reinvent the wheel in their small corners of the world.

Geographically, Australia is a long way away from the rest of the western world, but our death traditions stay closely linked to those in other western countries. Having said that, it is important to acknowledge our global society. It is often the practices of the non-western countries that are, in principle at least, closer to the traditional home death-care the grassroots movement is seeking.

My itinerary was 12 months in the making; it was constant research and planning and knocking on doors. I found it harder than some other Fellows because I was not just visiting universities, governments or private industries. Most of my connections were local contacts with individual groups and with local people who had not necessarily heard of the Churchill Fellowship. I did not have many meetings with big business. My focus is really on what the marketing gurus call 'experiential consumption' – how the end user (the person dying and their families) experiences the dying and death and their relationship to it through these alternative approaches and technologies.

INTRODUCTION

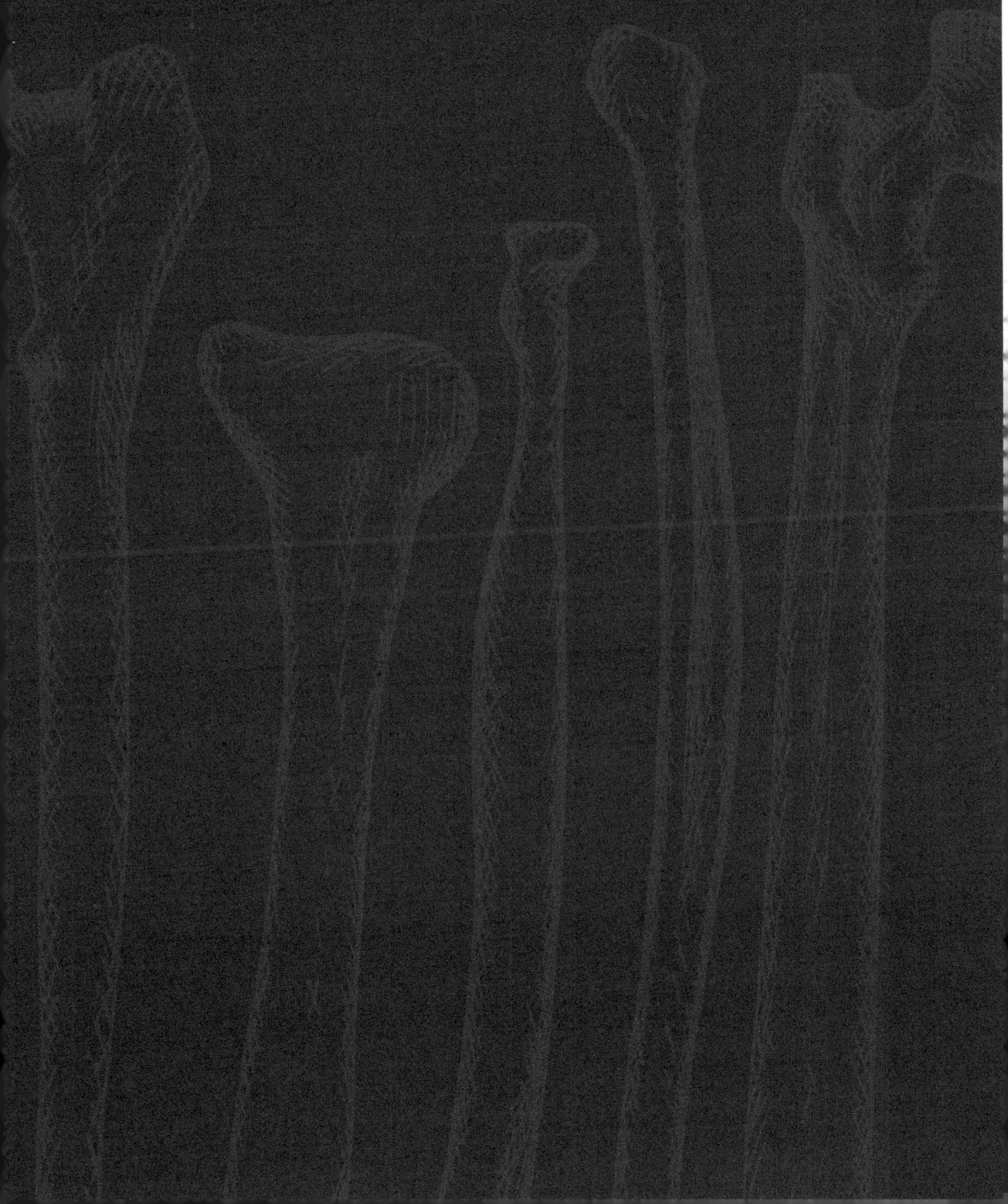

INTRODUCTION
AN AUSTRALIAN CONTEXT

It was four years ago that my friend Christine talked to me about doing a Churchill Fellowship. Our world is remarkably different now than it was then and we are still to see what the equilibrium of a post-Covid world will look like. Despite all the death work that has been done, it feels a little like it has only just begun. I learned so much on this trip and it is my hope that by sharing it with you, you can share it with others and we can change the face of death care across the globe, one conversation at a time.

'Auto-ethnography' is an approach to exploration and research where the writer is both the researcher and a participant in the culture they are observing. It is a personal approach looking at a culture and people. It was a very new concept to me but without knowing it, it was from this place that I travelled and learned, and from this place that I wrote my report, findings and recommendations.

We sit on a threshold in Australia in the changing relationship to dying and death in the western world. There is a movement to increase death literacy both on an individual and a community level, to enhance community capacity and social capital, to reclaim agency in how we care for our dead. I am part of the movement for change and this research project looked at a large number of different aspects of this change and the effects these are having on the space – through the disruptive influences of emerging technologies and approaches.

This project was in two parts, looking at both the different approaches to body disposal being suggested and developed in the western world and also at the different approaches being taken to death and ceremony. The purpose of this research project was to document and understand the different approaches and technologies and look at how they are changing the human relationship to death and ceremony with a view to enhancing the Australian experience.

I am keenly aware of the importance of my Fellowship report and what it means to the emerging grassroots movement looking to change our end-of-life-experiences. It is also entirely possible that this is the first time that all of these different parts of the changing landscape have been brought together in the one place. The final report was about 17,000 words and very well received, but I knew there was more to share.

In 2019 I sat in the Tasmanian Palliative Care Conference over two days and one of the presentations given was by the NSW Agency for Clinical Innovation. They gave us the following projections for Australia:

- By 2056 the Australian Death Rate will more than double to 320,000 p.a.
- 51 percent of all deaths will be those aged 80+
- There will be a 400 percent increase in the number of people over the age of 85.

More recently, projections have been slightly more conservative but they still predict a more than doubling of the numbers of deaths to come. According to the Australian Bureau of Statistics (ABS), Australia's population is projected to reach between 37.4 and 49.2 million people by 2066. There were 169,301 deaths registered in 2019, an increase of 10,808 from 2018. Our numbers of dead are increasing every year. According to the UN World Population Prospects, the Australian Death Rate will hit 8.741 per 1000 population by 2066 (based on a population of 49.2 million, that is over 430,000 deaths that year). What do we do with all of those dying people, what do we do with all of those dead?

Globally, conversations have begun about this trend, the wave of death (sometimes called the 'silver tsunami'), which is coming in the western world. There are medical and end-of-life professionals, academics and allied health workers the world over, all discussing this issue at conferences such as the one I attended; they are being engaged by both private industry and government to consider and formulate a plan as to how the medical communities, government services and the broader health sector are going to position themselves to respond to this and deal with it effectively.

In recent times we have had various Australian and international doctors, nurses and palliative care physicians, specialist and general, write books and give talks to support the idea that much of the caring around death is best done by non-medical people: the family, friends and carers (paid or unpaid) around a person dying.

They say that palliative care is not just about medical treatment, it is about grief and living well with illness; that dying and death, grief and loss are not just medical events, they are in fact social issues that have medical components. It is acknowledged now by palliative care physicians such as Dr Julian Abel, Professor Allan Kelleher and Professor Bruce Rumbold that successful end-of-life care requires more than just medical and clinical skills and approaches; much of what is required can be – and in many cases is – provided by community, family and other non-medical support.

In this context then, two things become clear. First, the people on the ground who are likely to be positioned for doing the work of caring for the dying – the end-of-life doulas, hospice volunteers, families and community members – are not the people being asked, given an adequate voice or valid seat at the table in the conversation about this growing problem.

Second, while as a society we are, in an albeit limited capacity, considering what to do with all the death we are projected to have in the next 40 years, we are not talking about what we are going to do with the increase in volume of human remains that will need to be disposed of as these people die. This is an incredible gap in the conversation and one that, if not addressed, could potentially cause dire logistical and social consequences in the coming years.

There is also another point to the Australian context of this investigation; end-of-life care and the ceremony and ritual of a funeral are becoming increasingly expensive and for many people a financially unviable and unattainable option. The latest IBIS World Industry Report S9520 into the Funeral Directors, Crematoria and Cemeteries in Australia notes, '*Consumers have increasingly opted for lower priced cremations over pricier burial.*'[1]

It goes on to say, '*Rising environmental awareness has also affected the industries' performance. Many consumers have been demanding more sustainable services, such as natural burials that use materials that break down faster than the traditional wooden coffins. Demand has also increased for reusable coffins...*'[2]

'Funeral poverty' has been identified in the western world as a pressing and growing concern and the reality of this is that people are either going into debt to cover the expenses of the farewell they would like to give their dead, or they are going without that farewell, traversing grief and bereavement without the ritual and ceremony designed to help people through the process.

In all of my reporting, I have tried to give as much context as possible about the people and the places that I visited. The reason for this is because death is a very different and unique experience on both an individual and a societal level and to understand how and why people die and handle death the way they do, you often need to understand a little about how they live as well.

This report concludes that we need to build new frameworks within which to navigate the dying and death of our communities. A shift in mindset with the accompanying economic commitments and investments is required to create better outcomes to meet the needs of the Australian Public.

There is a series of 13 recommendations raised from my research and findings for government, industry and community consultation and implementation. They include defining and giving form to the framework of the role of a doula and cementing the place for that role in end-of-life care, actively working to increase the death literacy of all Australians and bringing together the 'coal face' stakeholders to form both an Australian and a global response to the long term mortality projections that we face as a society.

Rebecca Lyons
Hobart, 2022

MY CHURCHILL ITINERARY

The following is a list of people I met with and places visited.

UNITED KINGDOM
30 August – 8 September 2019

Frome
Diane Roberts – Active and In Touch
Elaine Pugsley – Airbnb, Compassionate Communities
Bryce Tangvald – HOPE, Frome Area Christians Together
Tina – Hunting Raven Books Against Loneliness
Rose – Health Connector Frome Medical Centre
Julie – Area Lead for health connectors at Frome
Peter Macfadyen – Greenwood Funerals
Heather Massey – Rebel and home funeral guide
Howard Pickard – Resomation

Bath
The 14th International Conference on the Social Context of Death, Dying and Disposal Program

SWEDEN
9 September – 12 September 2019

Gothenburg
Rasmus Ringborg – Oscar Fredrik and Wahls Funerals
Susanne Wight-Masak – Promessa
Jenny-Ann Gunnarsson – Vila Begravning Funerals and Doula

CZECH REPUBLIC
13 September – 22 September 2019

Prague
Katerina Grofova – To the Roots, the Wood of Memory
Blanka Dobesova – To the Roots, the Wood of Memory
Eva Sejkorova – To the Roots, the Wood of Memory
Monika Suchanska – To the Roots, the Wood of Memory
Iva Sobothova – To the Roots, the Wood of Memory
Ivana Petrakova – Tranquillitas Funeral Home

ITALY
23 September – 26 September 2019

Milan
Maurizo – Onoranze Generali Funeral Home

Rome
Raoul Bretzel – Capsula Mundi

USA
27 September – 26 October 2019

Salt Lake City, UTAH
Royce Gibson – Memorial Lake View Hybrid Cemetery
Cole M Houghton – Tate Mortuary Funeral Home
Justin Crowe – Parting Stones
Joyce Mitchell – Funeral Consumers Alliance Utah

Minneapolis, MINNESOTA
National Home Funeral Alliance Conference
Sandy Sullivan – Resomation
Sarah Kerr – Healing Rituals
Pia Interlandi – Garments for the Grave
Ron Barrett – Anthropology at End of Life
Claire Turnham and Jerrigrace Lyons – Body Care 101 & 102
Lee Webster – Green Burial Council, National End of Life Doula
            Association and National Home Funeral Alliance
Claire Turnham – Only With Love, UK
Bob Jenkins – Let Your Love Grow

Los Angeles, CALIFORNIA
Birgitta Kastenbaum – LA Doula Collective Meeting
Lori Locicero – The Death Deck, Los Angeles
Ziri Rideaux – Friends Alternative Funeral Homes
Alua Arthur – Going With Grace, Los Angeles
Caitlin Doughty – Clarity Funerals and Cremation
Olivia Bareham – Sacred Crossings, Los Angeles

Crestone, COLORADO

Paul Klopenburg – Crestone End of Life Project
Alison Wonderland – Crestone End of Life Project
Gussie Fauntleroy – Crestone End of Life Project

Westminster, SOUTH CAROLINA

Kimberley Campbell – Ramsey Creek Nature Preserve

New York City, NEW YORK

Jeri Glatter – INELDA
Janie Rakow – INELDA
Katrina Spade – Recompose, Seattle
Amy Cunningham – Fitting Tribute

New Orleans, LOUISIANA

Valerie Armand – Doula and hospice worker
Brooke – Funeral director, New Orleans
Museum of Death
Lafayette & St Louis Cemeteries
Holly Pruett – Death Talk Project

MEXICO

27 October – 6 November 2019

Oaxaca and Mexico City

Vincenta – Airbnb
Viviana – En Via tours
Sylvia – Teoteatllin
Azucena – Mexico City, artist and journalist
Terresa – Teoteatllin

PART 1

BODY DISPOSAL

In this section I will explore the various methods of body disposal being developed and used around the world. They are all remarkably different and at different stages of implementation. I would like to note that there is one method that I did not include here and that is the Infinity burial suit, otherwise known as the mushroom suit. Despite many attempts to contact the designer, I was unable to speak to her and after my own inquiries, I became aware that the first burial using this suit which Infinity are currently following has not had the success in the way they had hoped.

Turn-off to the pyre site,
Crestone, Colorado, USA

Top: Bec in the Chattahoochee-Oconee National Park and surrounds, Georgia, USA

Bottom: A Catrina doll Bec made in a workshop in Mexico City, Mexico

NATURAL BURIAL FOR ASHES
TO THE ROOTS – PRAGUE, CZECH REPUBLIC
http://lesvzpominek.cz/

While I was in the Czech Republic, I spoke to a funeral director called Ivana, the founders of a not-for-profit called 'To the Roots' and a group of incredible women working with them establishing natural burials – Monika, Blanca, Iva, Eva and Katerina. I also spoke to many locals on my daily travels and in cemeteries and ossuarys throughout local villages and towns.

To the Roots (Ke kořenům) is a non-profit organisation that established The Wood of Memories (Les Vzpominek) inside a cemetery in Prague. Initially I met with founding members Monika and Blanca. Monika, who has since moved to Slovakia to set up a new natural burial project, was kind enough to travel back to the Czech Republic for a few days to show me around. Their model has been so successful that they have also expanded to open a new natural burial facility in the neighbouring city of Brno.

Monika did her tertiary studies focusing on natural burials and ceremonies and found that people were not being helped by the standard ceremonial process being offered in the Czech Republic, particularly in the city areas. Blanca has studied many eco-friendly aspects of life and death and is a passionate believer in a gentler, more personal approach to ritual and ceremony.

In Prague, only the government or a church can establish a cemetery; they cannot be established or managed privately. It was fortuitous that while they were still students, the then manager of a local cemetery approached them about starting a natural burial section in a part of a cemetery that had not been used in 80 years. The manager was quite progressive in his views, and supportive of their ideas, and after several discussions the project began. It was a success and continues under current management.

The Wood of Memories offers natural burial for cremated remains only, because Prague has one of the highest cremation rates of any city in the world. Monika and Blanca have friends who make eco-urns out of various types of paper

Plaques denoting burial sites in The Wood of Memories, Czech Republic

The clearing for ceremonies and land for burials in The Wood of Memories,
Czech Republic

which they sell to the public who seek out their services, or they bury ashes without an urn at all.

To the Roots are experimenting with a model of responsible burial and monitoring it to see how the trees cope. The burials take place about 2 metres from the base of a tree and they allow two lots of ashes per tree base. Once each tree has two lots of ashes at its base, there are no more burials at that tree for another five years. There has been no scientific investigation into the condition of the soil at this point, although the well established trees continue to flourish. To the Roots close for the winter – mid-November to March, as it is not good to disturb the tree roots when the ground is frozen.

To the Roots rent the burial spots to families for 10 years. After that time, the plots can be reused for another placement. Wooden plaques around the trunk of the tree mark where each person is buried; the plan is that the family will decide if they want that marker back after 10 years or if they will leave it on the tree.

There is a very profound need for the kind of change and healing being offered in The Wood of Memories. The Czech Republic is only 30 years out of Communism, with the anniversary of the Velvet Revolution being celebrated in November 2019. As a society, they have made huge changes to their social structure and way of life in the last 30 years, however there are still some things that are raw and there is a long way to go for many people to feel at peace with, and agency within, the changes.

This peaceful place that they have created lies in the same cemetery where many of the tortured male and female prisoners of the Communist government were buried, unceremoniously dumped like animals in a mass grave. Next to that section is a mass grave of all the children born to those incarcerated women. There is also a fenced-off area where all the unidentified people are buried – it has been this way for decades; in the same fenced-off space, machinery for ground maintenance is stored. It is easy to overlook and hard to see, unless you go looking for it, but it is also one of those things that cannot be unseen and it provides a stark contrast to the healing and light that people like Monika and Blanca are bringing to this space and their communities.

According to Monika and Blanca, the Czech Republic has one of the highest rates of direct cremation in the world. It sits at 50 percent nationwide and in Prague it is 97 percent. This is not a finance driven phenomenon: families

Stone centre where candle tributes are floated in The Wood of Memories, Czech Republic

come to The Wood of Memories after a cremation (whether or not they had a traditional or church funeral) because they are looking for a better grief outcome.

During the Communist times, all ceremonies, be they weddings, funerals or the welcoming of new citizens (baby welcoming) had to have political messages and rhetoric. When the Czech Republic became a democracy, they removed the political components of funeral ceremony but nearly everything else remained, including the procedures surrounding the ceremony for secular services. This makes the conventional ceremonies largely empty and impersonal, and Monika's research showed that people felt it did not help their grief journey.

Most of the funeral chapels were built under the Communist regime and as such they are cold and clinical places, the architectural style is aptly called 'brutalism'. Families get approximately 10 minutes with a celebrant before the ceremony where they pick music from a pre-selected list at the chapel and although some chapel managements will allow a degree of personalisation, others will not. This is the process for most people in Prague because currently, the majority of people are irreligious.

To the Roots are revolutionary in the Czech Republic because more than offering natural burial, they are working with families and community to individually craft personalised services for the interment of the ashes. One thing Blanca expertly encourages is for people to take their time and design something meaningful and personal; she helps arrange the exact ceremony they want.

Over time, To the Roots has developed rules for the burial ground – no plastic or cloth flowers, wrappers, ceramic statues, toys etc. and no candles. In the centre of the natural burial section there is a designated spot where people can light candles in memory of their loved ones; additionally they can write messages and peg them on a string hanging between two of the surrounding trees.

People in the Czech Republic are opening up to certain changes at the end of life, but only in very recent times. The way ceremony is done here in Prague is described as 'poor' and 'bad' by many people and through the natural attrition of the generations, attitudes are starting to change, and expectations are growing. People are keen for ceremony to be better. It is less about the finances and more about the grief outcomes. While in Australia there is a desire for better grief outcomes, a large push also comes as a backlash to unaffordable services as well.

To the Roots has never had someone come to them purely because it was an environmental choice. It is more about the aesthetic, the look, the feel, the personalisation and the desire for richness in ceremony to aid their grief. People from the Czech Republic are quite connected to the land for the most part and they have had a strong history of burial in times long ago and so they hold to the idea of burial within the earth as a final resting place as well. Ecological concerns are secondary to that.

To the Roots charge Kč4,000.00 (AUD$200.00) for the 10 years' tenure on the plot. They pass on the costs of flowers and celebrant without mark-up and they make a small profit on the urn sale, however their prices are not enough to cover Blanca's wages and meet the cost of the project entirely, so being part of a bigger cemetery means that their project is subsidised. With the new natural burial spaces being established, the pricing will be different with the focus on making them self-sustainable.

The size of each grave for a full-body burial is mandated under Czech Republic law. There are two sizes – adult and child – and each body must be buried in a hard wood coffin. Cremation must also be in a coffin. There is a coffin maker in the Czech Republic making eco-coffins but they are only for export at this

From top: A Post-communist grave in Prague;
and Communist era graves in Prague, Czech Republic

point as they are not legal to use and public opinion is such that people see them as being for poor people.

The idea of shroud burial/cremation is considered disrespectful and it is illegal in any case. In the city of Prague, cremation rates have risen exponentially, and it is only in other parts of the Czech Republic that full-body burial is still common but that is becoming less so.

The tending of existing graves is a well-entrenched part of the social fabric of the Czech Republic and it is largely done by middle-aged and older people. It is an obligation born of Eastern European influence but also of social expectation – there is a fear that a person will be looked down upon if they are seen to 'forget' their dead by not tending the grave. Each cemetery has intricate and ornate graves and there is a stark contrast between those that were placed during Communism and those placed or replaced after the revolution.

This dedication to the dead must be seen through the context of a society reimagining itself after brutal rule. There were expectations around tending graves and it was part of how being a good person was defined; to care for the grave of their loved one was the act of a good person and people want to be good. It is a hard habit to undo because of the implications of what not tending the graves would mean to the way they see themselves and each other. Some people only tend graves twice a year and replace plastic flowers etc. so they do not get too worn or shabby looking. Dotted throughout the cemetery are skip bins of varying sizes full of candles, fake floral waste and many rotting live flowers that have been recently replaced.

But there is another aspect to this constant tending to the graves of both full-body and ashes burial that has to do with grief and ceremony. The positive grief outcomes from the ceremony given at the time of death are negligible at best for people and due to that, people look for other ways to stay connected to the dead, perhaps as part of their grieving. The tending of the site of interment is a very effective way of addressing this need. This is perhaps why there are so many people placing ashes in marble topped burial plots in conventional cemeteries.

The younger generations are not taking on the social expectation of grave maintenance in the same way. The generation of those in their 30s and younger are not tending graves and To the Roots see a change coming in the Czech Republic where this younger generation will memorialise their parents very

Niche placements for ashes, in Prague, Czech Republic

differently. They expect a rise in the use of places like their own, along with columbarium and other more traditional ashes placements that do not require tending. One such option is the scattering ground, where for a very small fee the cemetery will scatter the person's ashes above ground on the grass. No ceremony or attendance or designated spot is provided.

It is legislated in the Czech Republic that funeral directors must be on call 24/7. They do not necessarily take the body from the place of death straight away though. If a person dies at home, they call the doctor first who comes and gives them the paperwork. Then families can call the funeral director; the time for this is not prescribed. Families can keep the body of their person at home, and this happened in the past, but it is not common any more as most people die in hospitals and facilities. By family request, the funeral director must return the body to the family home but this is not something usually requested since home-based body cooling options are limited.

I was privileged to speak with Ivana Petrakova, a Prague-based funeral director with Tranquillitas. Monika from To the Roots acted as interpreter, allowing me to gain a further insight into the funeral traditions in Prague.

Ivana has been a funeral director for 12 years. There are a few offices, called funeral agencies, of Tranquillitas around the city. This particular office does about 120 funerals a year.

Once they receive a call, they have people who will go and collect the body. They will move the body wrapped in a shroud, but that shrouded body is placed in a basic transportation coffin. The body is taken to an off-site cooling facility. Sometimes these facilities are outside Prague. Cooling facilities in the Czech Republic are largely privately owned: crematoria and funeral homes contract their services. There are several cooling facilities and each funeral company has their preferred provider.

Ivana confirmed that it is not usual to take the body home, but it is possible. In Prague, along with cooling facilities, cremations are also centralised: there are two private and one government owned crematoria. Many funeral homes use the crematoria under contractual agreements.

The preparation of the body is done by the funeral home staff. This is done at a separate site – each funeral agency has a central place for body preparation. The employees largely do the preparations, however if a family want to do this or dress the deceased themselves, they can at this site. This particular funeral agency has partnered with another company to do their body preparation, but this kind of co-operation between agencies is not usual.

In the Czech Republic, embalming is not a standard practice. Embalming only occurs if the family request it or for a crypt burial, repatriation, religious requirements or infection control reasons. Embalming is expensive, the average cost is approximately Kč30,000.00 (AUD$1,900.00) and it is based on the amount of embalming fluids used.

Stitching and the more invasive types of body preparations are done by the hospital staff if they deem them to be necessary (it is not done to everyone) before the funeral agency picks up the person's body, leaving only the basic washing and dressing of the body to be done by the funeral agencies. In the case where a body has undergone an autopsy, the funeral agency does not do much preparation, as handling the body is seen as unsafe.

Over time, there have been changes to how a body was prepared. Because not every mouth is stitched closed, in the past they would tie a scarf around a person's head to keep the mouth shut, but more recent legislation changes have

Bec with the team from To The Roots, exploring a new cemetery in Czech Republic

now made this type of 'body manipulation' illegal. It has been this legislative intervention that had seen other changes as well: the funeral agency used to be able to transport bodies just wrapped in a sheet (as they do in places in Australia), but now they need a transportation coffin. The regulation is getting more and more restrictive.

When someone dies at home the family have usually already washed and dressed that person before the funeral agency collects them. Viewings outside of this space or the hospital are not common. Here it is only legal for members of the public to view a body within 7 days of death, after that the only people allowed to see the body are the persons responsible for the funeral arrangements. In Ivana's experience, people do not ask for things to be different, they are all accepting of the process as it is. She is aware of the Jewish and Muslim communities here and their cultural practices but they have their own preferred providers of end-of-life and death care who know their customs and traditions.

Ivana has noticed that over the last 12 years people have come to have higher expectations of the funeral profession and this is reflected in the arrangements that they make. She works with families to produce a funeral invitation as is the custom here. Only celebrities have their funerals announced in radio, tv and paper advertisements.

For everyone else there is a printed invitation with an electronic copy which gets circulated to the family and friends of the deceased. It is customary to hang one up in the building where the deceased lived and other places of importance of social engagement. If the person was a resident in a nursing home, invitations are hung there too. Ivana offers a choice of poem, font, border and background paper for it to be printed on. There is also a variety of symbols they can choose to be printed on there.

The family spend 1–3 hours with the funeral director, arranging a secular funeral that will last for 20 minutes (a church service may go for an hour), regardless of whether it is a burial or cremation. In all of her 12 years only once has the family chosen to book a double 40-minute spot. In these short services, families do not usually speak, which means that there is very little personal content and no opportunity for people to pay tribute. If a family do not want a priest or a celebrant, they do not have any ceremony at all.

In regard to cost, Ivana noted that her prices are Kč12,000.00 for a cremation with no ceremony (AUD$750.00). If the family choose a full ceremony including flowers etc. the price is closer to Kč30,000.00 (AUD$1,875.00), which for them is about one month's wages. People from Russia, Ukraine and the Gypsy community all exclusively bury their dead but for everyone else it is cremation. The average coffin price works out to approximately AUD$300.00.

Their flower choices are limited to standardised arrangements which families choose from a book. These range from 35 roses in a coffin arrangement for AUD$162.50 – if the family chooses plastic flowers this is about half that cost – to approx. 60 roses for AUD$275.00. Their most expensive arrangements are wreaths and they are AUD$320.00.

Families are constantly tending graves with fresh flowers and trinkets and yet the funeral flowers are all disposed of rather than placed on the fresh grave after a burial. Ivana warns families that the crematorium and cemetery staff will discard the flowers immediately allowing them to make an informed decision in relation to their spending. Memorialisation of graves is not organised

A view of the chandelier of human bones hanging in Sedlec Ossuary, a
Roman Catholic Chapel found below the Cemetery Church of All Saints in
Sedlec, Kutna Hora, Czech Republic

through funeral directors here; families have to go elsewhere to do this and
it is done fairly quickly.

To the Roots are challenging the way they do burial in the Czech Republic
and the relationship people have to the cemeteries and monuments within
them. They find that cemeteries can act to shield us from the finality of death.
Cemeteries contain monuments of honour and respect for our dead, but they
function as a way to keep the dead with people, because up until now in the
Czech Republic, there has not been a better way. The bigger and the more ornate
the memorial, the more the distraction from the decomposing body beneath it.

A time will come when all of these monuments will be dust, the people they
are designed to memorialise no longer recognisable and long forgotten. To
the Roots promote this change in perspective and are finding that through
their eco-friendly approach the grief and bereavement outcomes for their
communities are much improved.

ALKALINE HYDROLYSIS

Alkaline hydrolysis is a process of chemical reduction whereby organic and protein-based materials are reduced to liquid. There are different ways of doing this using both pressurised machines with high temperature and unpressurised machines with a low temperature. I looked at two places providing this technology which they sourced from different suppliers, one was Bio-Response and the other was Resomation.

This is a relatively new method of body disposal, which is both a disruptive technology and a working technology. This process is known by many names including flameless cremation, water cremation, Resomation, Aquamation and it is legal in more than 20 states of America. Additionally, Resomation is being picked up now for introduction around the world.

Remains after the alkaline hydrolysis process of Resomation, Minnesota USA

Bec collecting human remains after the alkaline hydrolysis process of Resomation, Minnesota USA

AQUAMATION
TATE MORTUARY – UTAH, USA
https://www.tatemortuary.com/

In Utah I met with Cole M. Houghton, owner of the Tate Mortuary. He had worked there for 20 years before he became the owner. A few years earlier, Cole had settled on the idea of developing his own business – by establishing an alkaline hydrolysis facility in Utah. Part way through the setup process of doing just that, the opportunity came up to purchase Tate Mortuary, which he did, and he has now combined the two.

Cole calls his offering Aquamation and he uses a machine supplied by a company called Bio-Response.

With a view to offer his service state-wide, he has set up in such a way that all funeral homes in Utah could contract his service for Aquamation if they wanted to. Publicly, he made it a soft introduction to the market, but he offers alkaline hydrolysis as an option to every family he works with who choose cremation: water or flame? The uptake is steady and positive; he has been operating with it since November 2018.

While it was a large financial outlay, Cole believes it was imperative and he is committed to providing families with viable alternatives. He feels that there are some in the industry who are not progressing with the times and to stay current in today's society, funeral homes need to be open minded with families, responsive to their requests and dedicated to providing them with choices and options. He operates on transparency and honesty, so much so that his website offers any family a tour of their facility. Their facility is quite large – they have a chapel, viewing space, administration, both flame cremation and Aquamation, two fridges, coffin storage and mortuary space all on site.

Cole runs a completely self-contained model with his service provision all handled by his small team. He is the only funeral director there; he has two assistants and a person he can call on for casual work as needed. There are two office staff and a person responsible for pre-need and after care of the families. He is hands-on, doing all the mortuary work, embalming, funeral directing and cremations himself. He is lucky enough to live next door and since taking the place over it has become both his work and his hobby. There is always something to do.

There is a strong sense of family at Tate Mortuary – his office manager Shirley works in the same position her mother held for 40 years. Their clients are loyal to the name and the reputation of the business he has purchased, brand loyalty in this community is fierce even when people do not necessarily have good outcomes and he is keen to make every outcome a good one, through personal service and options.

Bio-Response have both high and low temperature/pressure machines. Cole runs the version that is high temperature and high pressure, although his machine is also capable of a low temperature process. Bio-Response do have machines that only do low temperature processes. The low temperature machines are unpressurised (that is, they work on atmospheric pressure) and as such cannot reach the high temperatures which it is argued by some to be necessary for the safe disposal of human remains.

The Aquamation process, according to Cole, takes about 12 hours for the low temperature process to fully complete. He has found that for the high temperature process it takes around 6 hours, sometimes less. His machine takes about 2 hours to fill the initial tank with water, where it undergoes a softening process before it enters the main unit.

Cole is still making adjustments to, and learning about, the process as he goes; gradually he is writing policy and procedures as to how it all works. He was also asked to present at the American Funeral Directors Association, with the hope that what he is learning can be passed on to others who take up this technology. Cole believes there are still things he can do to make this a slightly faster process, but in his current setup, completion of a flame cremation can be achieved in about one third of the time taken for his Aquamation process.

Cole finds it a delicate balancing act to successfully determine the amount of chemical required to be used when factoring in the types of preparation the body has undergone, such as embalming. Bio-response provide charts and guidelines for the amount of chemical to be used based on the weight of the body – and every body needs to be weighed prior to undergoing the process – however he usually uses a little more chemical than is recommended and at the time of writing was still fine-tuning the amounts. This is a manual process where he is required to physically handle and add the alkali to the water for each Aquamation process.

Aquamation, according to Cole, is a quieter and a less dangerous process than flame cremation but he is not yet sure about the running costs. There is upkeep for the plumbing, the seals and time to clean the machine between uses, and he also has to purchase the alkali. Flame cremators also have upkeep costs and at the time of writing he is not far enough along in his journey of offering this method of disposal to make that kind of financial comparison.

In his single flame cremator, Cole can put a body with a weight up to around 400 pounds (180kg). He has been told it is capable of up to 600 pounds (270kg) but he has not yet been called upon to do that. The maximum weight for Aquamation is about 350 pounds (158kg). If a body is larger than that, Cole says the body can still be loaded into the machine, however they may be required to run the Aquamation cycle twice. The need to run the cycle twice also exists in cases where heavy duty cavity fluid has been used in the preparation of the body because in both cases it will take longer for the body to break down. Indeed, even when this is not the case, some remains need to go in again simply because they have not been completely reduced in the initial cycle.

Cole took me to see the machine he uses and I saw the remains he had drying from a cycle the day before. The bones felt like chalk; they are pure white, soft, a little gritty and brittle. In Utah there is a law that human remains must be unrecognisable when returned to the family (meaning they cannot pick up the bones in their full state as I was seeing them) and so they are put through the same grinding processing as cremated remains before being returned to the family.

Walking into the room where the alkaline hydrolysis process takes place, the first thing I noticed was a warm and thick smell that I could not quite identify. It was distinct and unrecognisable and it reminded me a little of a kitchen. It was not either pleasant or unpleasant, simply different. Having been around death for a long time it was not something that I found difficult.

I asked Cole how other people reacted to it. He has had mixed reactions – it is unlike anything they have smelled before but most people are fine with that. And to be fair, death has a smell. Mortuaries and crematoria have a smell, and so does alkaline hydrolysis.

He showed me the difference between the metal implants from the water and flame processes. It was a remarkable difference: the ones from the alkaline hydrolysis process looked brand new and you could still read the serial numbers of the parts, whereas the others were burned and largely unrecognisable. After completing an Aquamation, Cole has made a practice of recording the serial numbers of joints and who they came from as another layer of ID if ever it was needed. There could even be potential for these joints to be recycled and reused, particularly in countries where access to this kind of medical procedure may be hard to come by or financially unattainable. It is an exciting possibility.

In Utah it is law that all bodies need to be in a silk bag for Aquamation. Cole has learned that the body needs to be prepared in a certain way to make the Aquamation process more streamlined. All pacemakers need to be removed and so does anything that may have been used for packing the body. It is commonly the case in preparing a body for viewing that the throat and nose cavities are packed with cotton as part of the body preparation regardless of whether or not the family is viewing – all of this needs to be removed.

When it comes to a body that has been autopsied, the internal organs are usually contained in a plastic bag which sits in the chest cavity. When this

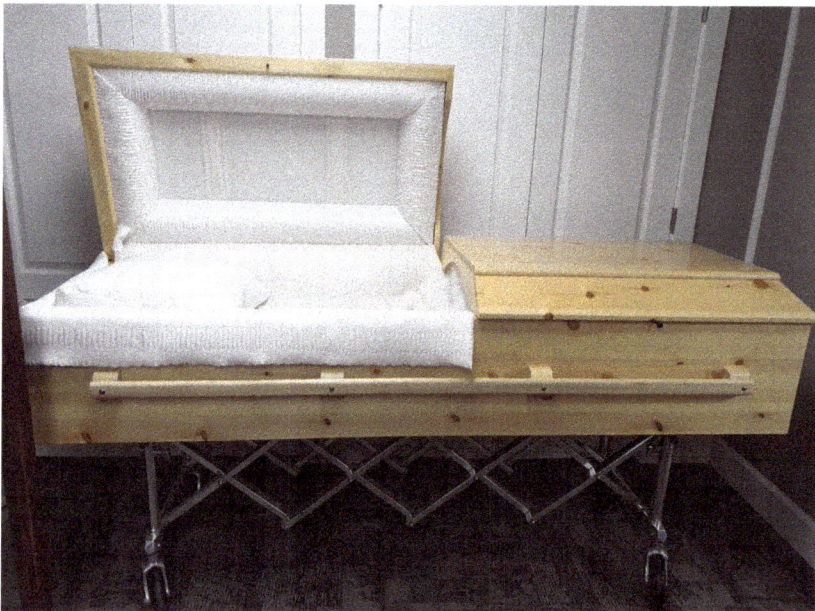

Above: Eco-coffin in the showroom of Tate Mortuary, Utah USA
Top right: A comparison of knee joints, one after an alkaline hydrolysis process (left)
and the other after flame cremation (right) at Tate Mortuary, Utah USA

is the case Cole needs to unstitch the autopsy incisions and the plastic bag containing the internal organs needs to be removed. All of the stitching is taken out and the organs placed into the cavity.

In the case of embalmed bodies, they leave in the plug from the trocar puncture site – that plug remains intact during the process and is removed after. In a climate that already embalms regularly (the USA has a high embalming rate overall), all of this may sound a lot of handling but Cole says it is not really a lot of extra handling. Over 50 percent of his families choose embalming, regardless of what choices they make around ceremony or disposal or how long it is until ceremony or disposal occurs.

Alkaline hydrolysis has been used to dispose of large farm animals for decades and the water has been used for irrigation and farming among other things. The process is really no different when used for a human, however the water is not just recycled in a farm setting. For Cole, the used water from the Aquamation process goes to a treatment plant and is recycled.

Cole had to work to get legislation passed to regulate this process; the Funeral Consumers Alliance and the American Funeral Directors Association each appointed an advocate to help educate and inform the legislature. The legislation passed on the second attempt. Like most things, alkaline hydrolysis was already technically legal (and therefore unregulated) so there was a desire to put an approved framework around it as a method of disposal for humans. This regulation governs the guidelines within which he can operate and develop his policies and procedures.

Utah is a very traditional place with a high religious demographic and Cole thinks it will be one of the last places to adopt some of the more radical changes we are seeing globally in relation to funeral services and body disposal. He is seeing more personalisation of the ceremonies themselves but there is little

From top: The Tate mortuary building from the outside and the coffin display room in Tate Mortuary, Utah, USA

impact from anything like home funerals or natural burials. I described to Cole how we handle the cooling of a body in Australia and what is being done in other places around the world. Interestingly, he says that based on those descriptions, home funerals would likely be possible in Utah because while they have a '24-hour rule' saying the body has to be refrigerated, buried or cremated within 24 hours, that would in all likelihood meet with compliance.

Cole says that the majority of services in Utah are religious, predominantly Mormon or Catholic, and burials outnumber cremations 60-40. Another shift he is seeing is away from actual churches as a venue. Even if families are still choosing religious services, they are more often now happening in chapels. He thinks this will become more the case as religious parents depart and more children start making secular choices

Another progressive decision Cole made, harking back to a time when it was more common than today, is to offer families who are choosing cremation the option of a rental casket. This is not uncommon in America although in Australia the practice has all but faded.

I was quite impressed with his rental coffins. They are ingenious. They are the same casket shape as conventional caskets (the standard in the USA is for a casket, not a coffin), but the corners come off with Velcro and then one end folds down allowing a cardboard tray with sides the height of the coffin to slide in. It slides out the same way and in doing so needs no disinfecting as the body has not touched the coffin. The cardboard tray can then be used to place the body in the cremator, or the body can come out of it and go into the Aquamation machine.

In Australia, we do not have the same ornate casket culture as they do in America. We still have coffins as a standard offering, whereas in most show rooms I visited in the USA, only caskets were on offer. All their caskets are much bigger than our traditional coffins in Australia and each casket has the half or full opening lids for viewing.

Cole has a very large showroom and another with the urns and jewellery. His caskets range in price from expensive to affordable, metal to wood and cardboard. One casket that took my eye was covered in velvet; this remarkable casket is called Fibre Board. Many of the caskets found in the USA are now made in China and shipped into the USA so they are by comparison substantially cheaper than what we would see in Australia for the same product.

Bio-response alkaline hydrolysis unit at Tate Mortuary, Utah, USA

The average funeral cost in Utah is USD$6,500.00 (AUD$8,975.00) and Cole's business is in the average bracket. He agrees that cost can be an issue and he is very aware when working with families not to add unnecessary burden to them. The diversification of service is a central focus for his business and helps him provide affordable options.

Cole represents a new generation of funeral director, very invested in the future which includes a firm commitment to this new method of body disposal. Cole says many people are finding a comforting, less harsh and confronting alternative.

RESOMATION
BRADSHAW FUNERAL HOME – MINNESOTA USA
https://resomation.com/

I was privileged to spend a day with Sandy Sullivan, the designer and owner of the alkaline hydrolysis process he calls Resomation. Sandy Sullivan met me at the Bradshaw Funeral and Cremation Services in Stillwater, Minnesota where they have been offering Resomation since they purchased their machine in 2013. Bradshaw have five funeral homes across the state and do about 1200 cremations a year. They offer Resomation along with contemporary burial and they outsource the process of flame cremation if their families choose that option.

It has been a slow process for Sandy. He has been instrumental in working to create the regulations and ensure legislative permissions in each state of installation, and now alkaline hydrolysis is legal in over 20 states of the United States. Sandy believes that now that California has been in progress since 1 July 2020, the other states will soon follow suit along with the UK and hopefully, Australia.

In the UK, all funeral homes are mandated by law to install mercury abatement systems to all flame cremators. These systems cost about the same to install as the flame cremator itself. This makes the option of buying a Resomation system (the machine is called a Resomator) an economically sensible decision for crematoria as a way forward, because the cost of buying and installing a Resomation system is similar to that of a flame cremator and no abatement is needed.

Currently, a handful of Resomation units operate across the USA. At the time of writing, three more units were being built to fill orders received and the company was preparing to build several more in anticipation of orders being discussed.

Sandy sees that in the near future his challenge will soon become logistical, being able to build the machines fast enough to keep up with the requests he is anticipating receiving. They have costed the machines competitively and if a funeral home or crematorium is doing 250–300 cases per year, they are likely to pay for the machine in 12 months. Sandy is dedicated to making Resomation a viable value-for-money service.

A Resomator only does a high pressure alkaline hydrolysis process, as he believes the science is not definitive regarding the effectiveness of how the low (or atmospheric) pressure machines deal with the remains. The Resomation machine goes to 150 degrees Celsius and the cycle time is 4 hours. He believes that this process, as he continues his refinements, could eventually become half that.

Sandy's background prior to starting Resomation had been in microbiology and sterilisation machines such as autoclaves, so when he had built his machine he commissioned similar testing to what an autoclave undergoes, to be done on his equipment. The results showed that the remains were beyond what is considered high level decontamination, there was in fact a 99.9999 percent reduction in the bacteria population. When considering the return of ashes to a family, high level decontamination is the standard that is required for human remains so Resomation goes above and beyond: remains from this process are sterile.

Much discussion has been made around human prions (a certain type of protein within a human body) and whether the high and low temperature alkaline hydrolysis processes deal with them effectively. Sandy has looked into this as well and found there is data for cattle based on a test done in Ireland to say that at 4 bars of pressure and 5–6 hours in duration at 150 degrees Celsius temperature, all the cattle prions are successfully dealt with. The Resomator operates at 10 bars of pressure and that same temperature, which he feels is more than enough to be satisfied of a successful outcome, however testing with human prions has not been done to his knowledge. Having said that, the University of California have done over 1200 of these high temperature processes in a Resomator, all without incident.

According to Sandy, the Resomation system is more expensive than the Bio-Response unit and this is largely due to the fact that he has developed the system to the point where the process is completely automated, reducing operator error and making the operator's level of exposure to the chemical negligible. It also means that the process of Resomation works first time every

From top: Bec collecting human remains after Resomation (alkaline hydrolysis), and the human remains after Resomation, Bradshaw Funeral Home, Minnesota USA

time – there is never any need to put the remains back in for a further cycle. Sandy has developed software allowing the option of selecting whether or not the body has been embalmed; this automatically adjusts the time and the chemical levels.

His original machines (such as the one I saw at Bradshaw) is an older design which has since had some improvements. Where the body going into the machine was originally weighed by the machine, this has been refined and the weight is now taken by a specifically designed automatic lifter, used to put the body into the Resomator. This is easier for the operator and streamlines the machine's operation.

Sandy's journey has been a long one and he is always trying to improve on the process and make the operational experience as easy as possible for the user. Sandy has addressed various issues as he has progressed, tweaking and improving his machine and the process to the point where he is now happily rolling out the current design.

The Resomator runs with two cycles for every process. The first cycle is where the reduction of the body tissue takes place and the second is a rinse to wash the bone remains, removing any remaining glycerol (which is a naturally occurring alcohol).

To begin the process, the body is placed into the chamber of the Resomator and the operator selects the cycle and enters the body weight on a control panel. The alkali and water are automatically added to the chamber based on this information. The amount of the chemical used in this process is about 5 percent by volume – the other 95 percent is water.

Start to finish, this process uses about 1500L of water, which Sandy says is approximately half the average daily consumption of a human. The water, once the process is finished, is automatically pumped to another vat. Initially, the pH level at the end of the process is approximately 12–13, so the pH is tested and treated until it stabilises at the correct levels (it needs to be less than 10) before it is released into the drain to re-enter the water cycle. The process to stabilise the pH takes about 15 minutes.

Recently the Dutch government commissioned a report determining that the water by-product from this process contains no DNA nor does it contain anything harmful and as such it is completely safe to go into the water treatment system.

This process of Resomation produces pure white ash every time. Once the remains come out of the machine they are rinsed again by hand. (Bradshaw do this to remove any residue left on the remains from the biodegradable plastic bag that must be used by law as a lining to their silk shroud.) Then they go through an artificial drying process in what looks like a little clay oven. Importantly, the remains can dry naturally, however the natural drying can take up to three days.

In Minnesota, funeral homes are required by law to have the remains available within 24 hours if requested, so the drying process needs to be quick. There is a thermometer style device, which tells them when the moisture contained in the bones has disappeared, and this is how they know the remains are ready for the next step. Once dry, just as in Utah, the remains are required to be unrecognisable, so they are put through the cremulator – a machine designed to grind the remains to 'ash'. When remains from an alkaline hydrolysis process undergo this grinding they produce a fine, pure white substance that looks exactly like cornflour and has a similar consistency.

Over the years Sandy has worked with the businesses who buy his units and as they identify needs, they are investigated and addressed. This was the case when the need for a machine to dry the remains arose, when a lifter to help load the body into the Resomator was required, and now Sandy is in the process of inventing a new type of cremulator that will capture all the remains without releasing particles as fine dust into the atmosphere. This will have a better and more desirable outcome for the family, health benefits for the staff and financial benefits for the business.

Another important distinction in the Resomation version of alkaline hydrolysis is that nothing metal has to be removed from the body. Bodies can go through the Resomation process start to finish even with a pacemaker – the working unit at the University of California reported that they have recovered pacemaker devices at the conclusion of a process which were not only intact but where the batteries were still working.

Alkaline hydrolysis, no matter the type, has an issue with the bio-hazard bags when a body has been autopsied; as previously explained, the morticians have to transfer the organs from the bio-hazard bag in the body cavity into a biodegradable bag so that it will dissolve in the process. The Bradshaw staff also remove all of the cotton or Styrofoam packing from the body, if any, that

Clockwise from left: Bec with owner and founder of Resomation, Sandy Sullivan; view from the viewing room into the Resomation room; the Resomator unit, Bradshaw Funeral Home, Minnesota USA

had been used in the preparation of the body. Cotton will not dissolve in the Resomator, nor any other alkaline hydrolysis process. At Bradshaw they have as a practice, stopped packing, stitching and using eye caps etc. as preparation of the deceased, unless family require it. Still they encourage viewing and also witnessing the body go into the Resomator (which is called a witness cremation), and in America this is not uncommon.

Sandy originally partnered with a private backer and then the Funeral Co-op before meeting up with Howard Pickard in the UK and partnering with his company LBBC Technologies (Leeds and Bradford Boiler Company, based in Leeds, UK) in 2008. Since that time, they have designed the machinery and refined the process to make Resomation a seamless and viable alternative to flame cremation. It is comparable to flame cremation in relation to time and turnover. Although the process at present takes 4 hours, the cost of installing his dual system (a system that has two machines that share infrastructure, allowing two processes to take place at the same time) is competitive with that of a single flame cremator with mercury abatement system in the UK. Running the dual system reduces the time required to get through a day's worth of cremations; this means that the time comparison is favourable.

Resomation uses potassium hydroxide as its alkali, in a liquid form, and this means that there is no need for a user to handle chemical powder. The chemical is piped into the facility from a tank with an outside valve. The software on the machine will tell the operator when the chemical is getting low so that a top-up can then be ordered.

Resomation is very inexpensive to run, there is no atmospheric pollution and it is not a labour intensive process – for those who do not want to be buried, it is the better alternative to flame cremation and it calls for a gentler handling of a person's remains with much less invasive preparation required.

There is a lovely narrative around the process of Resomation. This process allows the body to be broken down into the elements that created it and those elements are returned to the water cycle of life. Unlike other alkaline hydrolysis offerings, the water here does not need to be disposed of as waste, it re-enters the water cycle; this is one of the things that sets Resomation apart from the other offerings. Sandy has worked very hard to make this a viable way of the future. While it may not be directly value adding to the environment, it is a return to it in a largely harmless way which is an improvement on contemporary flame cremation.

CRESTONE OPEN-AIR PYRE
CRESTONE END OF LIFE PROJECT
(CEOLP) – CRESTONE, COLORADO USA
http://informedfinalchoices.org/crestone/

While I was in Crestone *(for more information about the town, see p.155)*, I spoke to Paul Kloppenburg, Gussie Fauntleroy and Allison Wonderland who are all volunteers with the Crestone End of Life Project (CEOLP). CEOLP have had many people ask about creating something similar to their offering, but to date no one has been successful in setting this up and Crestone remains the only volunteer-run, secular pyre in the country. I spent five blissful days with Paul Kloppenburg, the instigator and the now fire master, for the CEOLP.

There are two groups involved in Crestone when it comes to the end of life: the CEOLP which came first, and also Informed Final Choices (IFC). IFC was born of necessity and designed as a not-for-profit entity that could receive donations. The IFC is now focused on the educational arm of their work.

At the time of my visit, CEOLP had approximately 17 people with a wider network of 65–75 volunteers. In a town of 150 people (within a wider surrounding district of approximately 1600 people), this is a true community venture. CEOLP approach their work with a team-based ethos. There's a designated team for every stage in the journey of someone's after-death care, from care of the body to fire keeping and collecting the bones, and each team is made up of volunteers with an experienced team leader as guide.

Paul started doing outdoor cremations a very long time ago. He built a portable cremation pyre which he would haul around, towed by a big old American pickup truck. He would set up where he was needed and perform a cremation on the spot – the system has since been lovingly termed the 'port-a-pyre'. Paul had done five cremations over two years before there was any formal organisation put in place, government permissions or structure sought, even before CEOLP was born.

The first pyre cremation came about because a friend of Paul's, a Tibetan Monk, had wanted to be cremated outdoors upon his death and Paul agreed to make it

Top: A view of the township of Crestone, Colorado, USA

Bottom: Entrance to the Elephant Cloud Market in the township of Crestone, Colorado USA

happen for him. He obtained the permission of the property owner's association (for the local area in which his friend lived) and the only requirement they placed on him was to have a single working hose nearby *in case of trouble*. From then on and in the two years that followed, Paul learned as he went. He started to identify problems with the process and as there was no formal structure, there were instances where things went wrong. As he identified things that needed to be done differently or better, Paul learned how to refine the process.

Making my way around the town, I spoke to various locals. One Lady, Janti, told me she attended three of the first five cremations. She remarked how it was an interesting time to be a resident of Crestone because when she had cause to visit other towns in the area, if they came to know she was from Crestone the reaction she would receive was akin to – 'oh, that's the place neighbours burn neighbours...'.

Eventually Stephanie Gaines, another Crestone resident, and Paul decided there needed to be more organisation if they were to continue offering cremations, so they made the decision to temporarily stop doing cremations, to retire the portable structure, and they spent a further two years educating and advocating for a fixed public pyre as they worked to put all the structure and permissions in place.

Stephanie took the lead on this – she attended meetings, she lobbied and educated, she listened intently to all the community concerns and took the time to answer them one by one. They gathered scientists to talk about pollution effects and the concern of mercury among other things and in the end, they won permission to proceed. It was a long process but worthwhile; the site now holds the commemoration plaques representing over 65 people cremated there.

Approaching the pyre there is an information booth they have nicknamed the Celestial Bus Stop and it is full of information in relation to the pyre and the project. They have erected a sign on the road pointing to the pyre site. This service is known in the community now and people regularly visit the site. The sign itself was made by the local coroner, another indication of the widespread support that this project enjoys.

The pyre site is prepared the day before a cremation. The wood is stacked in a very particular way, in fact nothing about this process is left to chance. Paul has a very specific method for doing this that he has developed over the years, using the right type of wood, the right size of the pieces placed in a specific form to maximise airflow.

From top: The outdoor pyre circle in Crestone; and the pyre structure in
Crestone, Colorado, USA

On the day of a cremation, the body arrives at the pyre site at about 6.50am. The body has been dressed and shrouded, although the face of the person can be, and often is, kept visible up until the cremation is ready to start. The family and community carry the person down the procession path from the road to the pyre site and place the body onto the grates of the pyre. 7am is the time they begin the cremations because it must fit in with their fire permits and the wind strength and direction.

Every cremation is open to the community (unless the family want it private) and when the date is chosen, posters go up around the town so that people are notified. On the morning of the cremation the greeting team arrive early at the pyre site. They give each guest a piece of juniper bush as they arrive and instruct them to form a guard of honour through which the procession will pass. Sometimes they have a musical procession, sometimes it is a silent one, sometimes bells are rung or there is a single drumbeat. When it is time, the family and friends walk the body to the pyre site.

The site itself is contained within a bamboo circle. Inside that circle another smaller circle is marked out and inside that is the hearth. The inner circle is where the fire team work, and the outer circle is where people stand around to witness.

The procession walks through the guard of honour at the appointed time and into the circle. The body is carried on a single use bier, made by Paul, and placed onto the grate of the hearth headfirst and facing the mountains. After the family lays their person's body on the grate, the fire team stack wood up on top of the body, then family and the people attending all put their juniper over that.

The CEOLP have a recommended sequence of events for a cremation, but it always remains a family-led service. The main part of the service is generally a short and very personal affair, to fit within the burn times allowed by their permit, however the ceremony often continues in the circle throughout the cremation process. The space itself is considered by the community to be a sacred but secular circle.

Paul has built an altar for people to decorate and have personal items on display for the service and cremation. During the cremation people can spend time looking over these items, photos and treasures, sharing memories and stories about the dead.

There are three people in the fire team – one lead and two assistants, and it is their job to run the cremation. To be a lead you have to have had a minimum of 6–7 cremations as experience and be proficient in the operation; it can take years to reach this proficiency. Paul has designed tools for working the fire and a procedure to manage the fire as a process.

To start the cremation, the fire lead will hand the family four torches which they light from the incensor. This is a stand for the burning of incense which is lit prior to the procession entering the space. They then light the pyre from the four openings around the grate and once the pyre is alight, they lay the torches on the top. The torches are made from cheesecloth and ignite the pyre easily.

This is a very visible process; everything happens with people watching. The fire team need to be vigilant and prepared to work together to make it a smooth process and one that is not confronting for the onlookers. They add wood as needed to the fire, with one person throwing the wood in while another uses the push tool to aerate and another uses the hook tool to make sure the wood is in the right place. The movements are done in such a way that no one sees the body. Over time they have developed ways of dealing with the areas of the body that are the hardest to burn, without exposing the people watching to the visual impact of it burning. It is a delicate and highly skilled method of operation.

Kerosene is used as an accelerant to begin the fire. It has not been tested but Paul believes the temperature of the fire is somewhere between 1200–1400 degrees Fahrenheit. The burn lasts for about three hours. In that time, they use about a quarter of a cord of wood per cremation. (A cord is 4 feet x 4 feet by 8 feet long). The wood is a mixture of purchased, gathered and donated timber and is a mixture of different sizes.

Within 6–7 minutes of lighting, the flames will engulf the pyre if the fire has been stacked correctly. The first 12–15 minutes creates a lot of smoke and at that time of the morning it is wind from the mountains which usually blows it to the west. The fire is very hot at the start due to the accelerant – for the first 20–30 minutes there is a lot of energy and heat and the flames can reach up to 7 feet high.

The space for attendants is full at about 400 people, but no matter how many are present, people are often silent as the fire is lit, aware of the palpable energy and the sacredness of what they are witnessing. The flames are mesmerising, and people stare as they lick out the sides and dance above the hearth.

For the first hour and 45 minutes, the fire team will use a large shovel to manoeuvre the coals, piling them up at both the head and foot ends if they start to fall. Before the cremation begins, the family are given the choice as to whether they would like to keep some of the bone fragments intact. About 50 percent of the families do want this and if so the fire team keep aside the pieces of bone as they fall through the grate. This takes teamwork, it can be like a dance and ideally they are always in sync, each one knowing what the other is doing.

At about two hours and fifteen minutes the fire team need to disburse the torso to help it burn better. They do not 'rake over' or distribute the remains as is sometimes done in retort cremations, but they instead gently lift one side and then the other and as they do this, they add more juniper to the flames. This helps the burn and also means there is no smell. This movement of the torso happens about every twenty minutes then until it is no longer needed. In talking to people who have been present for cremations here, not one person has said they have smelled anything unpleasant.

About two hours into the process the post-burn team arrive. The fire team are relieved by them only when all the material on the grates has burned away and dropped through. The post-burn team stay for a further two and a half hours. Before they leave the site, they make sure the remnants of the fire and cremated remains are in two rows under the grate and they put a mesh cover over the hearth so that no coals escape.

Around midday the following day the cremated remains are collected and placed into the containers provided by the family. If they have requested bones, they are placed on top of the collected ashes. The volume of remains is about equal to two shoe boxes.

This kind of cremation has similar requirements to retort cremations (the standard indoor crematorium style cremation) where any pacemakers or other medical devices need to be removed first. Because the coroner is responsible for signing off on every disposition in Colorado, they have medical doctors who volunteer their time to come and remove them, along with any medical equipment like lines, bags and pumps etc. in preparation for the cremation.

Every 5-7 cremations (approximately every year), Paul undertakes maintenance on the hearth. He removes the fireproof bricks and gives the ventilation gaps and the substructure a good clean out. He uses refractory cement for the

From left: The incensor and fan used during the ceremonies at the pyre site; and the name plates on the poles that fence the pyre site, Crestone, Colorado, USA

repairs and maintains any that are in need. Every year the Property Owners Association send a fire inspector to inspect the site as well and give them a permit for another 12 months.

CEOLP do not own the title to the land the pyre is on, it is owned by the Dragon Mountain Zen Centre. CEOLP pay the Zen Centre a donation for every cremation that is done. This comes out of the money that families donate to them for their service.

Every year the wider volunteer group come together for a contemplative day there where they meditate, check in with each other and eat a pot-luck style meal together. They also have a set activity, which differs each year, that they do together and then at the end of the day they go to the pyre site where all the names are written down of all the people they have cremated since CEOLP's inception; they are burned with juniper. The team spend that time talking together and sharing stories about those who have died.

When the pyre site first started, they would give a donation to the fire service for each cremation and in return the fire service would attend. This relationship with the fire service has since changed as the fire service is now a paid one in Crestone, so the people at CEOLP leave it to them to decide if they feel the need to attend each cremation on a case by case basis.

Paul would like to see this kind of volunteer-based social model or cremation happen in other parts of the United States. The CEOLP model requires people to have registered with them in life if they are to be cremated at that site in death. It is a very specific case to be considered if people have not registered. People are required to live here for 3–4 months and/or own land here for that long and be registered. At the time of writing, they have 235 people registered for cremations. Every year they hold registration parties and they typically have a further 20–30 people sign up.

As a not-for-profit, CEOLP does not charge for its services but does ask for donations towards the costs. They also receive grant money from the county for the upkeep of the site. Funnily enough, those who donate their time and materials for this upkeep do it as a labour of love and they often do not accept reimbursement.

Fire bans are an issue – if there is a total fire ban then they cannot do a cremation but they do have a funeral home in nearby Alamosa, Rogers, who are happy to collect and refrigerate a person until the cremation can be performed. This is for a nominal fee.

One problem CEOLP have identified is natural attrition. Most of the volunteers are between 50–70 years of age and the physical side of the work, as well as the fact that they themselves are ageing, means that they need to bring in younger people to ensure it continues and also that those who have registered for this will have their wishes honoured.

Right: Memorial seat within which ashes can be interred, Lakeview Cemetery, Utah, USA

HYBRID BURIAL GROUND
LAKE VIEW CEMETERY – SALT LAKE CITY, UTAH USA

http://www.memorialutah.com/locations/lakeview/

Salt Lake City is a town that grew up around industry, mostly oil refining. A long time ago the area of Salt Lake City was part of a giant lake ringed by the mountains that stand guardian, towering over the city today. I visited the Memorial Lakeview Cemetery which is situated on what was once the shoreline of that ancient lake. No one knows exactly why, but locals tell me that thousands of years ago all of the water very quickly drained away. This is part of the reason why the mountains are largely bare, not covered in thick forest or bush. Once, they were not always so mountainous.

At first glance, Memorial Lakeview Cemetery looks like many lawn cemeteries, uniform rows of graves with standardised concrete plinths for memorial plaques. I met Royce Gibson, an employee there, who was kind enough to show me around. It had been a cemetery for many years. Memorial own five cemeteries and a few funeral homes all within a 30-mile radius of the city. They do Islamic burials in two of them and work with various other cultural groups as well. Across all their cemeteries they conduct about 1200 burials a year, only three of these on average are natural burials.

They have left many trees standing in groves throughout Lakeview Cemetery and from those they have identified a few groves that they are putting aside for natural burials. Lakeview Cemetery started offering natural burials 10 years ago when a University Professor who wanted a natural burial asked them to accommodate him. After some discussion, they agreed to allow it. They are now compliant with the Green Burial Council and are keen to stick to the regulations for what is considered a natural burial.

When it comes to the preparation of the bodies that are interred in their natural burial section, they allow the body to be disinfected and do not restrict the normal preparation funeral homes undertake when it comes to the after-death care of a body, but no harsh chemicals in relation to cavity fluids are allowed and no other preservation, including embalming, is permitted. A body can be interred in an eco-coffin or in a shroud and the graves are dug about 1.7m deep (deeper than needed). They are dug and back filled by hand, either by staff or the family. In winter this is difficult as Utah is cold and the first 6 inches or so of the ground is frozen, so must be broken by large crowbars before any digging can happen.

By stark contrast, in their lawn section of the cemetery, all the burials must be in single or double concrete vaults. This is not a legal requirement, but the policy of the cemetery management because it makes the maintenance of the lawn easier and the aesthetic appearance more inviting.

Lakeview Cemetery offers many variations of ashes placement in addition to conventional burials and natural burials. Families can purchase a spot in a public seat where ashes in their containers can be placed and the families can have input into the design and location of the seat in the cemetery. (Each seat can hold four lots of ashes). Ashes can go in the ground (single placements, in an urn), they can go in boulders (concrete, shaped and designed to take

From top: Stone above the communal vault where multiple ashes can be interred; and the first burial to take place in the natural burial section of Lakeview Cemetery, Utah, USA

two lots of ashes) and then Lakeview Cemetery offer options for people who cannot afford that kind of memorialisation. They have a communal vault (an ossuary) with a large stone set on top of it for small plaques. For a small fee the ashes are placed in a tube and dropped into the communal vault via a buried PVC pipe, then a small name and date plaque is placed on the stone. This is particularly lovely because it is a response to the financial strain people can be under. For those who cannot or do not want to inter the ashes in the cemetery at all (maybe they are scattering them or taking them home) they offer the family either a USD$300.00 (AUD$413.00) discount off a single vault ashes placement, or they have the option of having the deceased person's name inscribed on a cenotaph style monument in the cemetery for free – so they still have a place to visit.

Royce explained that in Utah, a complete home funeral would not be possible as they have a 24-hour rule for collecting the deceased. This seemed to be different from the information I was given at Tate Mortuary. I wondered then, how much of this rule is left to interpretation. We exchanged some information regarding home funerals and I told him a little about what is possible in Tasmania – he was intrigued and open to the idea.

Royce said that 60–70 percent of their funerals are still religious, largely Mormon, but also others such as Catholic funerals are quite common. All their graves are kept in perpetuity and he does not agree that there is a space issue in relation to land for burial. In his opinion it is more about how close we want to be living to the dead in our contemporary society. The graves at Lakeview Cemetery are not tended regularly by the majority of families, staff generally see more attendance from families at times that mark occasions, such as birthdays and holiday celebrations.

The lawns are managed on a strict routine – they mow every Tuesday and in preparation for that they remove all plastic ornaments and trinkets and flowers that day. None of them are recycled. There is a place they put the ornaments awaiting family collection and if they do not come within a week or two then they are discarded.

There is no lawn in the natural burial area, which is situated under a lovely thick canopy of trees. Because they are not using vaults in this section, there is a small amount of sinking that occurs in the grave sites but as the graves sink, they back-fill the plots immediately. The headstones are placed at the

Hybrid burial ground

Top: View of lawn section

Left: Bec standing beside a concrete vault used for burial of caskets in the lawn cemetery, Lakeview Cemetery, Utah, USA

head of the grave – and the people are buried facing east – but the headstone is turned the other way, so that people are not standing on the head of their loved one to read the stone, instead they stand on the foot of the grave below them. Nature has already begun to reclaim their earliest burial sites and apart from keeping the stone visible, they intend to let it become wilderness once again. There is not talk here of reusing the burial sites.

Lakeview offers a look at what full-body natural burials can be inside existing cemeteries. It is incredibly important to be able to strictly adhere to the requirements of natural burials, maintaining the integrity of the site regardless of the current low numbers of natural burials requested. Eventually, it may even become the only way burials are conducted if the public continue to push for these changes.

NATURAL AND CONSERVATION BURIAL
RAMSEY CREEK PRESERVE –
SOUTH CAROLINA, USA
http://memorialecosystems.com/

Ramsey Creek Nature Preserve is a short drive from the small town of Westminster in South Carolina. Nestled among trees and abounding in old-fashioned southern hospitality, Ramsey Creek is a burial ground which is the first of its kind in the world. Ramsey Creek is the brainchild of Dr Billy and Kimberley Campbell. Dr Billy is both the town's FP (similar to an Australian General Practitioner) and a staunch advocate for environmental preservation.

Ramsey Creek is the closest I have come to seeing a natural burial ground in a landscape akin to the Australian bush. It was exciting to see because it works so well. The Ramsey Creek site is steep in some places with many different parts – a meadow, a creek, a clearing with a beautiful chapel, scrub bush and thickets of ferns and trees.

Burials occur in both forests and meadows; the south-eastern meadowlands (prairies and savannas) are among the most endangered habitats anywhere in the USA. Around the trees, the graves are mounded up high, which means that they do not need to bury so deep. Even graves that are more than 10 years old are still mounded high, meaning either there has been a lot of back filling or (more likely) there has been minimal if any sinking of those burials. Ferns grow on graves and in the sunnier places, wildflowers. There is wildlife in abundance. Each grave has a stone marker but this is left to return to nature.

Each section of the ground is marked with numbers on a wood marker. High quality golf carts allow access all over the grounds and are also used in moving the bodies from the carpark to the actual burial sites. Families are permitted to use these carts to access the more difficult sections of the burial ground when visiting as well. There are gravel paths in the main area and then less developed paths that have been formed through the bush over many years and since been covered in leaf litter. It makes for a beautiful walk. The trails are named, and the site has been mapped for ease of access.

Entrance to Ramsey Creek Burial Preserve, near Westminster, South Carolina, USA

What makes Ramsey Creek truly unique however, is that Dr Billy and Kimberley Campbell have also pioneered the concept of conservation burial. This is a revolutionary model of operation that actively works to preserve the flora and fauna of a site. It works like this: if a 10-acre block of land is acquired, a portion of those acres would be set aside for natural burials. Most conservation burial grounds are over 15 acres in size and most use the majority of the property for burials, but at a lower density than found in a conventional cemetery. In the old section of Ramsey Creek they have 33 acres for burials and there will be a total of only 1500 body burials over that space. (Contemporary burial grounds can have 700–1000 bodies per acre).

The management of conservation burial sites usually follows a not-for-profit structure. The profits made from the plots sold in that natural burial ground go not only into the maintenance of that land, but also to habitat protection, restoration, and the acquisition of new land. Ideally this new land would be neighbouring the existing ground, and that creates wildlife corridors (large tracts of uninterrupted land that wildlife can move between), which expand with each new acquisition. Their burial grounds have detailed multi-seasonal and ongoing botanical surveys to ensure that their activities contribute to ecological restoration of their lands. If the management structure is a for-profit model, they operate in such a way that their ethics and values include the drive to be socially responsible.

In his blogs, published on his website Memorial Eco-Systems, Dr Billy Campbell discusses the most effective and ecologically friendly methods of natural burial and what happens at Ramsey Creek. Plots are dug 3–3.5 feet (just under one metre) deep and wooden chocks are used to keep the casket/body off the ground in the grave to allow for aeration. They ensure that the disturbance to the soil is kept to a minimum so as not to impact too heavily on the ecology of the site. Vegetative matter such as straw, pine, ferns and flowers, is used to line the bottom of the graves, providing carbon to balance the high nitrogen levels during decomposition. Any tree roots inside the grave are pinned down with u-shaped pins rather than cut.

Dr Campbell coined the term 'burial sticks' to refer to dry limbs from the forest floor which can contain the spores of fungi. They place these burial sticks in the grave to allow for oxygen to circulate. This aids decomposition by providing channels for water and nutrients to help against the formation of adipocere (a waxy substance that can form in the presence of much body fat, slowing the decomposition process). Finally, organic vegetative material is added to the graves.

Dr Campbell notes that many green technologies, such as the eco-style urns and mycelium suits, are inherently flawed. He is a realist. The restoration of land is an intergenerational project; old growth forests do not grow quickly. Conservation burial takes old burial ethos and applies modern conservation science.

When considering the conservation of any tract of land, a conscious decision should be made around the removal or maintenance of non-native species – what is native to an area? Where do you draw the line? Should bees be introduced to help pollinate the flora? Dr Campbell feels that conservation burial is not about returning to a pre-colonisation ideal of what the land should be but simply a promoting and encouraging of native species. If something was once an introduced species decades ago but now grows wild, is it worth the harm to the

Natural burials at Ramsey Creek, South Carolina, USA

ecology to achieve its removal? Likely it is not, but all of these considerations are made in relation to the management of the land at Ramsey Creek.

There is also the very human benefit of making this type of place available to a community. According to Dr Campbell, there is medical literature supporting the idea that walking in natural non-urban areas has a positive effect on cognition and depression. He says,

> *The main rationale for conservation burial is that the projects can be trans-generational and personally transformational-and exist long enough (centuries) to restore damaged landscapes: it is impossible to grow an old growth forest in 40 years. Families and communities are connected to these spaces...*[3]

In 1996 Kimberley and Dr Campbell formed the company Memorial Eco-Systems and opened Ramsey Creek Nature Preserve in 1998. Dr Campbell was the first to come up with the idea of conservation burial. At the time, they were garnering investors and looking for land when Kimberley called the South Carolina Cemetery board, only to be informed that the board had closed, and they did not know where the powers over cemetery governance had been placed. In their county, Oconee County, there were no zoning restrictions and so Dr Campbell's idea was to position the cemetery within the landscape – close to places that have been 'saved' already, or are managed with conservation in mind, to create bigger wildlife corridors and ecological diversity.

Initially, they had chosen a different site but when that fell through, they decided to gift their privately owned land at Ramsey Creek to the company Memorial Eco-Systems to begin the project. They started with 36 acres and an additional 38 acres have been purchased since. They had only been open two weeks when their first burial, a stillborn child named Hope, came to them. That burial was a healing experience and set the tone for their work going forward.

What Dr Campbell has created over the years of working on this conservation burial model is a set of core values and principles, which can be adapted to different places and environments. Ramsey Creek is a for-profit model and they pay a not-for-profit conservation land trust called Upstate Forever to hold their standards and govern the management of the grounds. Because of the conservation easements held by Upstate Forever, they are not only accountable in the land management but the land is also in perpetuity – the land will continue to be managed the same way, with the same ethics, long

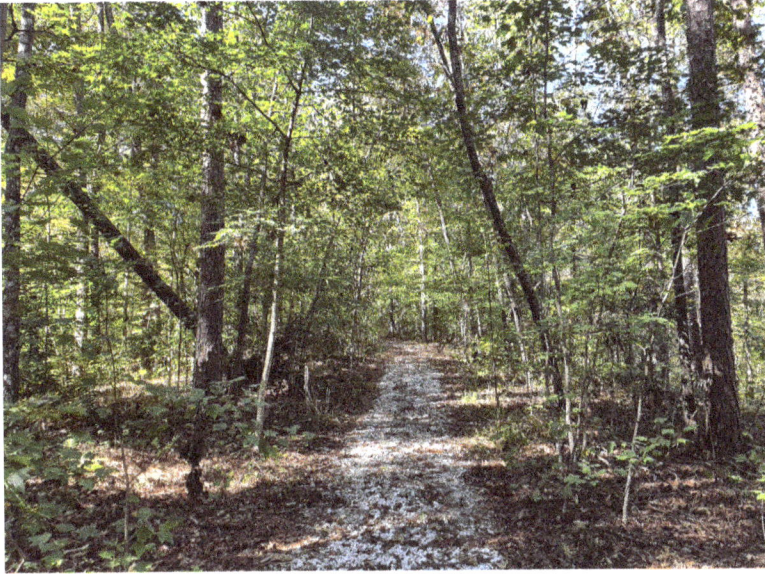

A path through the conservation burial ground at Ramsey Creek, South Carolina, USA

after Kimberley and Dr Campbell have died. Interestingly, whether the setup of the burial ground is for- or not-for-profit, they all generally work with land trusts to help maintain the integrity of the site.

The grounds at Ramsey Creek have paths laid out with markers, many of which were done through the aerial survey, following the lay of the land. A section of their preserve called the Midden Path is full of rubbish and glass bottles. This part of the preserve was originally part of a farm that practised poor soil conservation, resulting in deep gullies in the landscape. At the time, the advice from the county to the landowners was to fill these gullies with trash to stop the erosion, and that is what they did. After the farmers filled the site with trash and waste, they introduced a quick growing plant called Cudzu, which is Japanese in origin and can grow up to two feet a day. In no time, this covered up the rubbish.

When the Campbells started preparing the land for burials and were slowly trying the remove the Cudzu, they discovered dozens of projectile points and stone tools in the area, along with all the rubbish and glass. Consequently, they do not bury in this area now and that is how it acquired its name, the Midden Path. They do remove the rubbish as it comes to the surface naturally, making the decision that to dig it all out would disturb the ecology even more.

All of this tells an even bigger story: they are not just repurposing the land – from a mine to a forest – but they are reclaiming and rehabilitating the land as well, from the purposes and people who once exploited it.

In understanding and defining natural burial, language is a difficult issue. For many in the end-of-life space, we are constantly defining these old things that are new to the modern society and having to reintroduce them as concepts. In relation to burial, Kimberly feels that we need to be discussing 'contemporary' not 'conventional' burial. If we refer to standard burial practices as conventional, it implies that natural burial is not conventional, and it actually is – it is also traditional.

She also tries not to say the word 'cemetery', as it conjures up the images of the types of contemporary burials that people are used to, so what they are doing is not a 'cemetery': it is a nature preserve which is a multi-dimensional and accessible place of nature within a community. This and many other points form a part of the natural and conservation burial education they offer across the United States.

Kimberley and Dr Campbell have been working with and talking to other land trusts across the USA. They are often looking for ways to raise funds and working with natural burial ground owners and advocates. More and more opportunities are arising to conserve areas of land. This approach to conservation is gaining traction and around America the Campbells are increasingly being consulted in relation to conservation approaches.

Over the years they have been active in the Green Burial Council and they are pioneers and authorities in this space. More recently they have helped form a Conservation Burial Alliance. They have also done some consulting with the Mt Elliott Cemetery Association in Detroit who wanted them to look at one of their 10 sites they were considering for a natural burial area.

According to Kimberly, Dr Campbell describes the hybrid cemeteries as having a 'vegan section in a Brazilian meat market'. In the case of Mt Elliott, they had a separate 30 acres tract of land where they had planted a screen of evergreens, behind which they had been dumping excess dirt from the contemporary graves. Upon inspection, this turned out to be the best place to start a natural burial section, in line with the natural landscape and embracing the local flora and fauna. While surrounded by conventional burial, they are seeing the value natural burial can bring in the land and to their community.

From top: The Chapel where ceremonies are held at Ramsey Creek; and views within the Ramsey Creek burial ground at Ramsey Creek, South Carolina, USA

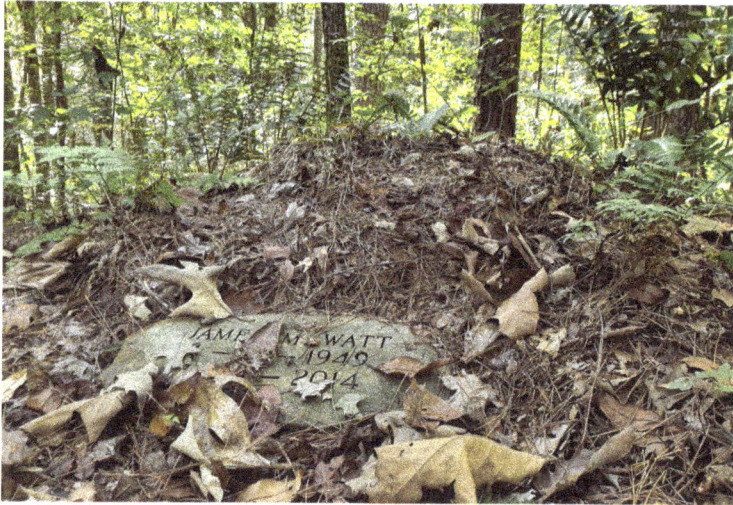

Views within the Ramsey Creek burial ground at Ramsey Creek, South Carolina, USA

The Ramsey Creek preserve began before people had ready access to the internet, in 1996. It took them two years to get ready. By the time they opened in 1998 they had a website and although the connections were slow and the graphics clunky, it was an important start for them as people could follow their work from the beginning. They had to mark out the land for burials by using a compass and a map and they hired a plane with infrared to do surveys and made their original grids from there.

Over the years, Kimberley has found that some funeral directors operate with policies that do not represent the actual legal rights of people, not necessarily allowing a family to do all they could towards the death care and burial for their person. Most of the burials they have at Ramsey Creek come from funeral homes, where the businesses have handled the deceased rather than the family.

The Campbells make a point of speaking with the families and giving them instructions and guidelines about what is and is not acceptable for natural burial. They use bio-glues, wooden pegs instead of nails, salvaged wood where possible etc. in the coffin but they are often reliant on the funeral director to comply with this. Having said that, at Ramsey Creek, as in many other places offering natural burial, they will always preference family requirements over the rigid rules. If a family were making the casket and they used metal screws to hold it together, that would be acceptable; the process of having made the casket is more important than a few screws going into the ground. In this way they are making a mindful choice to support capacity building in their community.

Dr Campbell speaks with medical authority when he challenges the necessity of embalming and other heavy preparations. He educates families about the more natural ways of doing things. Over time, the funeral directors the Campbells have been involved with have begun to see a real drop in rates of embalming. The drive for community education and a desire for a more ecological end is having an impact.

Kimberley feels that in western society, we have lost the skills of caring for the dead and we need to reclaim them. The missing piece is where families and communities spend the time to look after their loved ones after death. Often families are not given all the available options at the time of someone's death so when it comes to choosing a disposal method they turn to the contemporary industry for this.

There needs to be more education around the alternatives and more services that fit with the ethos of the DIY space. Increasingly people are seeking a different way of doing death that offers a greater connection with nature and with each other. The rhetoric about our final act being a gift to the planet needs to maintain its authenticity; through active participation in the natural burial process, families find a new kind of peace in their grief.

HUMAN COMPOSTING
(NATURAL ORGANIC REDUCTION)
RECOMPOSE. SEATTLE, WASHINGTON USA
https://www.recompose.life/

I did not physically visit Recompose in Seattle as the site had not opened at the time I was travelling, but I was lucky enough to interview Katrina Spade by phone. More recently I have attended Recompose presentations online, in Australia and the USA. The Urban Death Project was founded in 2014 as one of a few iterations of human composting, or natural organic reduction: a process that was championed by Katrina Spade. It has been a passion for Katrina for over a decade and her full-time work since the founding of Recompose in 2017.

Katrina models her approach to this work with the basic tenets of transparency and clarity for all people. She believes that everything about this project should be considered and deliberate. This translates into her vision for Recompose: everything from how her team will arrive at the family home, transport the deceased and how they will be handled upon arrival at the facility. She is considerate of how this entire process will be experienced by families and to that end she looks at everything with a focus on design and experience.

Recompose is a death care company run by the inventors of recomposition, a process of natural organic reduction which gently converts human remains into soil. They have been in operation since 2020 and have served over 50 families. Due to restrictions of the current premises the public are not allowed to visit this site, however once their final home is complete Recompose plans on being able to have families attend for the interment (called a 'laying in') and be able to visit when their person is there. They are raising the capital to build the first stand-alone and user friendly site.

Many years ago when Katrina was in graduate school and studying architecture, she began thinking about the funeral industry and the way humans interact with the end of life. She started out thinking about the options available to her at her own death. She became aware of research having been done with composting livestock and her idea grew from there.

After a few designs she arrived at the idea of a vessel-based approach to human composting. This process sees a body placed into a vessel on a bed of woodchips and compost material. It is a controlled environment and it takes about a month for the entire remains, including bones, hair and teeth to break down. They then cure that material for a further two weeks. There is no DNA left at the conclusion of the process, no tissue nor any trace of the remains.

The development of the vessel system was long and detailed. They were looking for a way to make the vessels and facility translatable across various locations, and it has paid off. Katrina is excited by the options opening up in relation to having this system implemented in urban areas around the United States. Recompose has filed patents for international use, but for now they are concentrating on the USA. This process is available in Washington, and at the time of writing it is expected that it will soon be available in Oregon, Colorado and California.

Recompose have worked hard to enact legislative changes to allow their method of body disposal. All of the trial and testing has been rigorously done and their proof of concept has been well established and documented. They have raised funds through ethical investors who are aligned with their values. Katrina maintains that while they are a corporate venture, they will maintain a strong sense of corporate responsibility and to that end they are not willing to align with businesses that do not fit their ethics or the way they see Recompose operating. There is a strong sense of integrity and civic accountability in every aspect of what they do.

Katrina wants this process to be completely interactive. Once the final facility is ready, they anticipate welcoming family and community into the space at the time of the laying in, and at any times family choose to visit while their person is there as well as at the end when the compost soil may be collected.

If a family does choose to take the soil home, the staff at Recompose instruct them on how to spread the material and mix it with soil to add the compost nutrients to the existing soil. There are best practices for handling the compost that have been developed throughout their trial processes which are shared with the family.

Just as with ashes, there are some families who never collect the soil or do not feel as though they want to take it home. To address this they have partnered with a local 700 acre conservation project at Bells Mountain so they are able to offer families another option for the compost use.

Top and inset: The design concept for
a purpose built Recompose facility;
a Recompose burial

Right: Katrina Spade,
founder of Recompose

Images Courtesy of Recompose

The process of Recompose focuses on both the disposal of the body and the journey to it and the Recompose team are actively increasing the death literacy of those they interact with. As staff at the facility, they engage with people often long before their deaths and at the time of writing they have over 800 'pre-compose' clients – that is, clients who have pre-paid for the Recompose service. They are building community capacity through their work.

Katrina has put a lot of thought into developing a family centred framework for ritual from the start of this journey. Katrina and her team were not just looking at providing a composting process – they are aiming to offer a holistic approach, considering everything that they may need for the system to work and deliver on good grief and bereavement outcomes for families. Katrina intends for this to be a process wrapped in dignity, with marks of honour such as the ringing of a bell when a body arrives, as a mark of respect, signalling to everyone in the building that it is time to welcome someone.

Another option Recompose intend to incorporate in their facility is a visiting room for the laying in where the family can help prepare the vessel with woodchips etc. Families will be able to help with the laying in and as mentioned, they will be free to visit over a 30-day period if they choose. Families will also be able to add their own ritual and ceremony to this, working with Recompose's own funeral directors. Importantly, Recompose has made it so that families can deliver their person to the facility without the aid of an external funeral director.

When dealing with something completely new, there is usually a measure of new language that is required to discuss it. There are definitions to be made and ways of describing actions using existing language with which a context can be created for people's framework of understanding. For the process of natural organic reduction which they offer at Recompose, the language has evolved over time.

Katrina explained that she used to talk about human composting; it was a known term for a new concept. She has never been afraid to call this process anything other than what it is, even when people found it difficult. Her mum came up with the term 'Recompose' which they have adopted in their approach to branding and it is now the name of the company. In defining this offering, Katrina shies away from words that belong to the funeral industry. The language of the contemporary industry is too often structured in a way that allows people to deny the reality of death and she wants to be as clear and transparent as possible.

Early in the development phase, the team at Recompose did a life cycle assessment of the process, taking into consideration everything from travel to the production costs of things like coffins, and of course the burial process itself. They found that the carbon footprint of cremation, and contemporary burial were roughly the same. They then compared those carbon footprints to that of Recompose. The result was significant: with 1.4 metric tons of carbon per person better off by the process of human composting. A big portion of this was that there is no coffin required for neither interment nor transport.

One question often asked, how can the soil be used? The soil at the end of the composting process can be used to grow ornamentals, trees, shrubs etc. but they do not promote the use for the growing of fruit and vegetables – not because it is not possible nor because there is any potential harm from it – but sadly, because of the language. Some in the media have been quick to get distracted with false and sensational claims guaranteed for internet traffic and these, however inaccurate, are more harmful to what they are trying to achieve in terms of community education.

The science shows what the composition of the 'non-remains' are at the end of the process. The nutrients are not unique or different, person to person, and they are not different from most other composting materials. It goes against the idea that we are all individual but it is a reminder that we are returning the elements that we borrowed to make our bodies back to the earth we borrowed them from.

Katrina is keen to help get the Recompose system off the ground in Australia and around the world, but first they are working to introduce it to America. She knows the death space is watching this, though she was not really aware that others were looking too. It was a surprise for her to hear that people ask me about it when I go to do talks. Once the first purpose built facility is operational, it will likely be a quicker moving process to establish similar facilities elsewhere.

PROMESSA. GOTHENBURG, SWEDEN

http://www.promessa.se/

Susanne Wiigh-Mäsak died in September 2020. Originally Susanne and I had scheduled a few days together in 2019, however after a series of communications we agreed on a day and time for a single interview. As per her request, I sent my questions prior to our interview time. At the time of writing, the project is currently ongoing without her. The following is a report based on our conversation, and was written prior to her death.

Susanne has had approximately 40 technicians working on her process of Promession over time, and it has now reached a point where she feels that no further adjustments are required. Susanne has said that they have tested over 100 pigs and are satisfied that this process is now ready for human 'caretaking'. However at the time of writing, no human trials have been done, meaning that a proof of concept is not there.

According to Susanne, two countries are in the process of education about Promessa with an aim to begin work towards implementation in the near future. She states that some countries have completed legislative changes and are in the phase of education to implementation; she hopes Australia would soon follow.

Currently, as both a company and a philosophy, Promessa rejects the notion of *body disposal*. Susanne prefers the term 'caretaking', because she feels that the word 'disposal' had a negative connotation. She explains that there is something profound to be gained from looking at the body as food for nature and that it should be treated this way in our language as well.

Susanne is a biologist who started her work over 30 years ago, looking at kitchen waste and composting in day-care centres. She found herself considering what would happen when we died and so she started talking to an industrialist about this idea. With his encouragement she invented the process of Promession and eventually patented it.

Promessa is built on two fundamental ideas. One, that no poisons should be put into a body; and two, that the body is a gift to nature. Susanne hopes that the natural burial movement will eventually include the remains from those who undergo the process of Promession. Susanne had many questions about the process of decomposition in natural burial grounds and the actual value those remains add to the soil as they turn to liquid during the decomposition process. She felt that the fluids of the body during the decomposition process would hinder the nutrients returning to, or adding value, to the soil.

Promession is designed to deal with all organic matter, including humans. Once she had the concept, Susanne said she spent the next two years speaking with around 1000 people in relation to her idea – only three of them objected. In 2003 Susanne started a not-for-profit so that people could show their interest in Promessa. (Still today, people can go to their website and sign up as a 'friend' of Promessa and receive updates about its progress. At the time of our interview she had interest registered from people in 100 countries.)

The process of Promession is designed to imitate what happens in nature, but by removing the liquid component and breaking the body down to smaller pieces, with the intention being that it makes the return to the earth easier and more complete. At the end of the Promession process there are dry remains which do not thaw and do not turn to liquid, as she said they do in the natural burial process – they can be stored on a shelf. Susanne describes the process of Promession like so:

The body is first frozen for a minimum of three days. After that time, the body is placed in the purpose built machine and the machine removes the body from the coffin. The coffin is shredded and added to the remains later in the process. The body undergoes a flush or spray of liquid nitrogen making it brittle and then a vibration process turns the body into small pieces. The remains of the coffin are then added to the human remains – this is optimal to aid the decomposition once in the soil. From here, the next stage is the removal of all liquid – creating dry remains. These combined remains are then put into a second coffin they have specifically designed, and the staff of the facility/operator of the machine will fasten the lid on with a glue that Promessa will supply to the owner/operator of the facility.

Susanne created this concept as an automated process to limit handling and operator input. All the operator has to do is load the machine at the start and

From left: View of the Göta River estuary; flowers found in Gothenburg, Sweden

glue the lid on at the end – all other stages in the process outlined above are done in the machine she calls the 'Promator'. The process is called 'Promession', the facility where this takes place will be called the 'Prematorium'. Once the remains are in the second coffin, they can be stored that way, unrefrigerated, for an undetermined length of time. 'They will not smell', she assured me, 'as they have been completely dried.'

The Promator machine is designed to run 24 hours a day and will be capable of processing 6–8 bodies per 24-hour period. As with cremation, pacemakers should be removed first. (In Sweden the hospital does that when they receive a body for storage anyway and hospitals are often used for this step.) All other metals and any metal contained in the construction of the first coffin are separated during the process in the Promator machine. The machine is capable of separating out metal as small as 0.1mm. Originally Promession was designed for burial, however if the family want 'ashes' back, Susanne said she had also acquired a compact cremator to put the dry remains through a cremation process which can produce ashes for the family. According to Susanne, this cremator creates about 350kw of heat from the process (because the remains contain about 70 percent carbon) and Susanne expects that this can be retained and used as an energy source within the facility.

When it comes to the actual burial in the ground, Promessa stipulates that it must be done a particular way. Their specially designed 200mm x 800mm x 144mm coffin is to be buried as a shallow depth burial; the grave is 50cm deep. By burying dry remains this way, Susanne said she expected they would be completely decomposed in 18 months. For safety, she said the grave plots would not be reused for a minimum of three years after which time the plots could be used and reused over and again in three-year cycles.

In her years of considering contemporary ways of dealing with human remains, Susanne said she had come to the conclusion that the process of cremation is actually a 'boiling' of the bodily fluids, and it is through this boiling process that the body is reduced. She felt that if we were to talk about cremation in this way people would probably be less likely to submit themselves to it. Language was important to Susanne, who has had to develop new terms to describe her process. She acknowledged its power in the framing of the discussion around death and the handling of the body.

Susanne said Promessa was working with 10 Promessa Ambassadors around the world. These are people who have paid to receive the training from Promessa about the process in order to return to their communities and raise awareness and support for the introduction of this method into their country. She noted this is a long and slow process.

Given that this concept is completely new, Susanne felt education and engagement were the best approach, with a focus on education as a first step to reduce any potential resistance. She wanted Promession to be met with welcoming attitudes when introduced and the stakeholders – the family, funeral directors, clients etc., to be well aware of what it is and how it works before it is made available as a process to families.

In talking to Susanne about the dry remains, there was a caution around the safeguarding of these remains. She explained that because it is still pieces of human in a shallow depth burial, Promessa has a metal net that is intended to be placed over the grave to anchor it into the earth, staying there for three years. The idea behind this, according to Susanne, is so that lunatics do not dig up the remains or take trophies from it. She suggested that exhuming a body that has undergone the Promession process would be different from digging up a regular dead body because in the case of the regular body, the remains would smell and be visually displeasing from decomposition, whereas these dry remains would not. The use of this net is non-negotiable: the remains must be buried as she outlines above with the coffin glued shut and the net in place. There is to be no room to move in how this process proceeds. Consequently shroud burial is not at all possible and you cannot bypass the need for two coffins.

I asked Susanne about how families would experience this, she said family engagement would be as it was with any other process – they could keep the body at home, wash and dress the person etc., in line with the laws of the country. In relation to families witnessing the actual Promession process, it would technically be possible to build the machine with a glass panel for families to see, however the spray of liquid nitrogen creates a snow like mist, and this would inhibit visibility. She said that there might also be an option for families to see the remains before the lid was glued on but she was very hesitant to consider this other than by direct request. She also made the point though, that the body is food for the earth and should be treated accordingly; she is a big believer in families approaching after-death care with this in mind.

Susanne said that after many years of discussion, the Swedish Church had recently come on board with this as an option in principle. It had been a long time coming but she was hopeful that they would soon be able to press on with the implementation of this process as another option for handling human remains in Sweden.

There is a cost to production in this process as with most others. The production costs of liquid nitrogen are minimal and none of the liquid nitrogen Promessa uses is produced exclusively for them. A company in Stockholm produces liquid oxygen for hospitals and facilities and liquid nitrogen is the by-product of that and only about 40 percent of that by-product can be sold due to lack of demand. The rest is 'left over' and so Promessa has arranged to procure it and the manufacturer has been happy to provide it to them.

Susanne said that the Swedish authorities spent a year looking at her research and development in relation to public health and the safe handling of remains, and they have concluded that they see no 'waste risk' at all with this method of 'caretaking'.

When asked about cost, Susanne felt that once this is made public, it would be comparable to the cost of cremation wherever it is introduced. That is another of the roles of a Promessa Ambassador; they provide Promessa with information about the market costs and trends and provide the community with education in order to garner support for the process.

This project has been over 16 years in the making and a working model is still to come. There has not yet been any trial of human proportion and it appears as though any introduction of this process is a long way off, if it gets there at all. This is not indicative of the time, effort and funds that have been put into the research and development of this concept, but despite all this effort and dedication it has not come to fruition. It is a long way from being considered a viable alternative to flame cremation.

It would be interesting to see the science behind the Promessa model, how the remains respond to burial and the energy cost for the process. One thing is for sure, this technology is creating a disruption in the end-of-life space and really has people talking about end-of-life options.

PART 2
DEATH DISRUPTIONS

A death disruption is a new development in the defined end-of-life space that causes people in and around it to stop, think and potentially reconsider. It could be the introduction to a new idea or way of looking at something, a new use or interaction with a product, an entirely new design that calls old ways into question.

The end-of-life space in Australia has never seen as many current death disruptions in such a short space of time as it has at the moment. Many of these are coming from overseas and following trends that are occurring elsewhere. Doulas and home funerals are disrupting influences on the contemporary funeral industry, as is natural burial and the various methods of body disposal outlined above.

There are many disruptive groups emerging into the public arena and many have gained international traction such as the Death Café movement, Death Over Dinner, Order of the Good Death, the Modern Mortician, Chick and the Dead, Garments for the Grave and the Collective for Radical Death Studies. In this section I would like to focus on some new international products that are bringing a disruptive influence to the end-of-life space.

CAPSULA MUNDI
RAOUL BRETZEL – ROME, ITALY
https://www.capsulamundi.it/en/

I met with co-creator and designer Raoul Bretzel in his studio in Rome. Immediately I was struck by the calm composure and a remarkable authenticity of this deep-thinking man who along with his design partner Anna, has thrown himself into this work. First and foremost, Raoul is a designer and primarily his designs have been furniture and bespoke pieces, always with an eco-friendly approach.

Capsula Mundi started many years ago when Raoul and Anna had the opportunity to present their design work at an Italian Young Designers Fair. They had participated a few times previously and by their third year they decided they needed something unique.

They started discussing how the wood in coffins is used for only a few days and yet there is a huge energy cost to their production. They decided to create a concept that was an alternative design for a coffin, but also something with an entirely new aesthetic and made of more environmentally friendly material. They ended up redesigning the concept of burial.

Quite a lot of time was spent considering the shape of their design and eventually they settled upon the egg – when considering death they saw this as a symbol of life and rebirth. Their intent was that by using this shape people could be prompted to reframe and rethink their relationship to mortality. The concept of using remains to aid the growth of a tree's life was also an important part of their development. They see it as having the potential to create a cultural change, a shift in thinking about how we view cemeteries and further, how we remember the dead.

Raoul explained that generally, tombstones are chosen for the most part because people think they will last forever. While I believe he is right in this, what I saw in many of my travels (not just in Italy) is that often they do not last, and many lie crumbling in disrepair within a generation or two.

Graves that have a 10-year limit on the Isola di San Michele, Venice, Italy

So with the drive for something lasting, one of the attractions of this concept is that people have the option of leaving something that does not need upkeep while also adding value to the environment.

The Capsula Mundi receives a lot of press, many positive and some critical reviews. It is important to note that Capsula Mundi began as a concept, pitched at a design fair. No one then knew the attention it would receive. It certainly achieved the goals of making people reconsider mortality and disrupting conventional practice. It was designed to get people talking, specifically about the 'cultural knot' that death has become and the feelings of taboo which often accompany it. The Capsula Mundi was not originally designed as a product they intended to make or market themselves. They considered the feasibility of it and they had spoken to a biodegradable plastic factory to develop a polymer, but they never intended on being the manufacturer themselves. It was only due to the huge international interest and demand in the concept, that they did eventually investigate the production and finally began developing a smaller version of the Capsula Mundi for ashes.

Years on, they are now making and supplying people around the world with this product for retail as urns for interment of ashes. The demand has not stopped. Again, due to the many requests they regularly receive, they are considering entering into the research stage for full-size human burial.

In Italy, space is a huge issue. In the cities there is a 50/50 split between burial and cremation. Only in the rural areas where tradition is stronger and space is much less of a problem, do burials outweigh cremations. For this reason, interments in the cities are limited to strict lengths of time. Where the burial is directly into the ground, there is a 10-year limit. After that time, the remains are removed and the family can choose to have them either cremated with the ashes placed in a wall niche or in the case of fully decomposed remains, the bones can be placed directly without a cremation into a wall placement. There is not an option to keep paying for more time when a plot's allotted time has expired as can be found in other countries.

The vast majority of Italian in-ground burials are made in concrete vaults and it is inside that vault that a solid wood casket, sometimes with a metal lining, is buried. This is the same if a full-body interment is done in a wall or above-ground crypt. In the case of these kinds of burials the body is often embalmed and the remains are not removed until 30 years have elapsed. At the end of that time the same options apply – the remains are usually cremated and placed in a niche. The only exception to this is if the family purchase or build a vault house that can hold many members of the one family. They are forever, although the management of some cemeteries may require some kind of ongoing payment and the obligation for this payment is inherited through the generations.

In Milan, I tracked down an English-speaking funeral director. Maurizo had been a funeral director since 1979 with Onoranze Funebri Generali, who are well known for doing international repatriations. Maurizio often works with the Embassies of Philippines, Ecuador, Peru, Sri Lanka, Dominican Republic, London and Geneva in repatriating the dead. The business has one doctor in Rome and another in a place near Verona who do their embalming as required.

Embalming is not as common there as it once was. Years ago, the majority of people who died in Italian cities such as Milan were buried as full-body

Capsula Mundi, a burial urn for ashes. Rome, Italy

burials into crypts and walls, and as such they were always embalmed. Now, this is a less common practice in the cities because the bulk of people here are cremated. Body burials and crypts have become too expensive.

When a person is cremated there are many options – ashes can be kept at home, buried in a cemetery or scattered in nature. If a family choose to bury the ashes in a cemetery, this is also a burial for 30 years and after that the family have the option of taking the ashes home. Funerals are generally held in churches, if not then in a chapel at the cemetery – Maurizo suggests that only about one in one hundred families would not have a service or ceremony. Over the years ceremony has encountered very little change: it is still largely traditional, often Catholic. Maurizo has noticed some very small changes – fewer flowers being ordered, for example – but there have been no major cultural shifts to speak of.

An average service in the city is expected to last for 30-40 minutes, no more. I asked about what this kind of traditional ceremony did for the family – how it helped their grief. Maurizo met me with quite a candid response, he said it really didn't. These services are only the beginning of the journey to addressing the pain of grief. He noted that more recently, an increasing number of people are using psychology services to help them with grief as well.

In Maurizo's experience, the average time from death to ceremony is only two days. He explained that the speed is due largely to the fact that many hospitals do not have refrigeration, and so there is an expectation that the body needs to be dealt with quickly. They have something called a 'frigor box' which provides a kind of industrial cold room storage. He described it as a box that goes over the coffin. According to the website I found they can make them to order for all kinds of purposes. They can also be used in family homes.

There is certainly a growing push for the option of doing things a little differently, some of which can be attributed to Raoul and Anna and disruptions such as their Capsula Mundi. Raoul sees the Capsula Mundi concept of a vessel that re-joins people with the earth and delivers their ashes (or body) back into the cycle of life. As an idea that allows humans to feel closer to nature, Raoul hopes this progresses to people paying more respect to the earth. Raoul says that he sees the Capsula Mundi as a natural biological consequence to life.

In a place where cremation rates are high and where ceremony is both traditional and lacking in choice, the addition of a new interment option such as the Capsula Mundi for ashes is an important and new approach to the narrative that frames it.

The original design has been shown around the world, conceptualising a body buried in a foetal position and a tree sprouting from it. The design that they now have for ashes is the same shape and is made of biodegradable plastic. They have experimented with the material to look at how it breaks down and they have received certification that is required in Europe to show that the raw material is biodegradable. It takes between 1–6 years to break down, depending on the soil composition and temperatures.

Raoul is aware of the issues with ashes being incompatible with some plants and damaging to some tree roots and to this end he has experimented with this product to observe it as it degrades. He has found that the egg first weakens and then cracks which means that the ashes come into contact with the soil slowly. He suggests burying the Capsula Mundi 80cm deep, allowing 40–60cm for the roots of the tree that is planted on top of it. I asked whether this could be a shallower burial if seeds were planted on top instead of a full tree and he said that would be fine.

Anna told me that her motivation for this work comes because it is about her life and her future. She is so happy to be creating something that she intends to be both for, and also part of, a social change that is being embraced worldwide. They are a small company and every decision they make is a considered one.

As Capsula Mundi expands, Raoul hopes to be able to work with local communities to eventually make this product locally in many countries, out of native materials. Obviously, each material as it is identified will need to be tested, but he wants to engage with local communities to be able to manufacture and distribute this product on a local level. This is based on empowerment and capacity building within local communities, as well as reducing the carbon footprint of freight.

Raoul has found that the people who talk to them when they are presenting on this concept find that they feel easier talking and thinking about death. Overall, they feel lightened to be able to think about a more natural end of life because they can remove the heaviness of the cultural taboo that has been put on the topic. That makes it all worthwhile.

SOLIDIFIED REMAINS
JUSTIN CROWE – NEW MEXICO, USA
www.partingstone.com

Justin is invested in creating real life solutions to problems that have been identified by academics while also addressing the problems experienced by bereaved families. Justin came to this work as a designer, through the death of his grandfather.

He started researching death and loss and how others around him were reacting to it and found a common thread. The problem is this: people hold the ash of their cremated dead in high esteem. It is a valued possession for many people and yet there are very limited options for what to do with ash and virtually no way to interact with it in a permanent and meaningful way.

Justin maintains that human remains are not inherently scary, but the form they come in is – a corpse or ash. The model used by funeral directors for their business and service provision to families was built largely around burial. This is now very out-dated and cremations are on the rise. Cremation has ruined that burial-based model and no one knows how to fix it. Moreover, in the last 25 years the cremation disruption has been growing.

Justin became interested in the death care industry years ago, taking on the role of managing editor of www.connectingdirectors.com. Quite quickly, he saw the need for broader thinking. He started going to funeral industry conferences and realised that all of the options for what to do with a person's ashes, such as glass, diamond, jewellery, keepsake urns etc., are all just bandages for the actual problem – only a part of the ash is used for these things and the rest has no use, there is still no way of interacting with them.

In order to address this, he received a grant from Los Alamos National Laboratory to investigate a new way to process the cremated remains and solidify them – all of them – into stone-like remains that can be then given back to the family after cremation. With this process, families no longer receive ashes – they get 60–80 'stones'.

Solidified remains are a brand new form of human remains, only entering the market in late 2019. This process was three years in the making and has the potential to vastly change how we interact with the remains of our deceased and in doing so change the way our grief and bereavement outcomes are experienced in an extraordinarily profound way.

Justin invented the term 'solidified remains' to name the finished product once the ashes have been put through the process he has pioneered. The ash is purified and through a ceramic firing process, the end result is the production of stone-like remains. The energy cost of this process is comparable to that of creating a coffee cup. At present the turnaround time frame is about three weeks, however the actual process can be done in less than three days and once it has been streamlined, three days will most likely be the standard turnaround. The cost for a set of stone from human remains at the time of writing is USD$695.00 (AUS$968.00); the costing for international customers has not been determined.

Justin is now in the process of community education in the USA about this process and its accessibility. There have been well over 3000 lots of cremated remains solidified since trials began in January 2019 – both in the pre-launch phase and since. During the trials, local Santa Fe animal shelters provided the ash for the research and development phase and Molecule Design (NM), Regency Mortuary (AZ) and Cremation Society of Illinois (IL) were the test market.

From its inception, there has been equity built into this service. This publicly available process is not accessed exclusively through the funeral industry, and therefore it cannot be controlled by one industry or entity. Justin has made this available to industry, private and public sectors equally. Funeral homes can offer this service at the same cost as the public are able to receive it should they choose to engage with Parting Stone directly.

Solidified remains are a platform for personal memorialisation. They can be completely interactive. Stones can be carried, decorated, painted, engraved – there are endless memorialisation options. When Justin and his team ask people what they have done with the stones received, the most common thing they have been told is that they share the solidified remains with family and friends.

People want to share the essence of their loved ones with other people and standard cremated remains make it difficult to do this elegantly. Multiple

Parting Stones made from solidified remains – Images courtesy Justin Crowe

customers have also told them that they take the stones to therapy as a way of dealing with the emotional processes of grief and bereavement. People feel these stones connect them to their dead in a very unique and tangible way.

Justin hopes that by opening up people's thinking about what can be possible with human remains, there will be many opportunities for others to follow with new developments as well.

Given that this is still very new, there are aspects to this process that are still being discovered. At the time of the interview, Parting Stone had the remains from alkaline hydrolysis and anticipated that the process would work perfectly. Interestingly, every person's ash comes out as a different colour, but they are still collecting data as to what causes this.

Justin believes that solidified remains will have a positive impact on families and enhance the grief and bereavement outcomes for people. His goal is to make solidified remains the preferred option for receiving cremation remains worldwide.

LET YOUR LOVE GROW
BOB JENKINS – USA
https://letyourlovegrow.com/

Bob Jenkins was a funeral director before he decided to create a product that would allow ashes to return to the natural environment in a way that would benefit, instead of potentially harm, the eco-system. It has long been known that ashes in their raw form are of no benefit and in some cases are harmful to the environment and yet a great number of people still choose cremation, so the ability to embrace the narrative of returning ashes to nature is appreciated by many.

Bob's journey started when he worked with a man to come up with the idea of turning ashes into potting mix for plants. That venture fell through and so Bob and his wife, a pharmacist, decided to continue to pursue the idea but with a completely organic approach. To begin, they got ashes from a pet crematorium and started experimenting with them but found that their plants were dying. So, they put together a team of scientists to look at why, and the result was that they established just how toxic ashes can be to the land. Since then Bob and his team have developed 'Let Your Love Grow', a product for pet ashes and more recently, another version for human ashes.

Let Your Love Grow is a compost, such as what you would buy in a garden centre. His end product has been tested and is successful as a compost for all manner of garden uses. The growing of hemp, fruit and vegetables is possible and further, Bob says that the products of those plants are safe for humans to consume.

Through his research Bob found that the bone fragments contained in ash must be disbursed; root stems will turn away from cremated remains because of the sodium content. This is why other products that offer combining ashes with the growth of trees will not work with young plants. He says the biodegradable urns do what they say they do – they break down in the earth. But the ashes that are left form a concentrated mass which is nothing but a toxic addition to the environment.

Bob says the sodium level in ashes is 200 to 2000 times the level of healthy soil and the pH is so high that it can also have a detrimental effect on the environment. Established trees are durable, and the root system will just grow around the ashes if left in raw form – it does not add value to the soil, but it will not kill the tree either.

Concentrated ashes absorb water and become like concrete under the earth. During his testing, Bob worked with a cemetery and was able to show that after decades buried, the ashes are still present in a solidified lump. It is only in the dispersing of the bone content that the remains will begin to break down. Let Your Love Grow addresses these bone fragments, lowers the pH levels and changes the sodium content of ashes, treating the ash to make it a viable nutrient and food for plants and trees.

His product is made in mass amounts and then aged. He takes compost from waste materials all over the world and then works it to get the bacteria levels right before it is aged. Bob uses packaging that is natural, no glue and only water-based ink. Conscious of the environment, he assured me that the process has a low carbon footprint, the only energy that it uses in the making of the product, is in the machinery used for the digging and making of the compost.

Most of the sales of Let Your Love Grow are to families who have ashes at home and don't know what to do with them. He has found that by offering this to people at home they find it a therapeutic experience because it is a 'doing'. They get the product, mix the ashes in by hand and then use that material to plant and grow things. He has also had families use his product to treat the ashes and then give little bags to the attendees at memorial services to take home with them for their gardens, thereby spreading the benefit to the grief and bereavement processes of many people.

Let Your Love Grow can be mixed, planted and buried into the earth on the same day – they have a 30-day dissolvable container which can be used, or it can go direct into the ground. If ashes are to be scattered however, they first need to sit after the mixing for 3 months. For 10 years Bob and the team have been using this process and never had a family come back to say it didn't work.

Bob had worked for the American SCI (the same company who started what is now known as Invocare in Australia through a mass acquisition of funeral homes and then the sale of the same to the Macquarie Bank), and he describes himself like a reformed smoker from big industry. He makes his products available to cemeteries, industry and public alike. The pet version of Let Your Love Grow is readily available, and it is planned that the human version will be sold direct to the public in Australia when available as well.

Bob and the research team are now turning their attention to whole body burial and how to make that process more organically acceptable to the earth. They are looking at creating a version of their product which would be able to introduce the bacteria back into a body which in theory would allow the components of bodies to break down in the earth rapidly, breaking down the body from the outside in. The idea is that when this introduced bacteria meets the bacteria in the body, they feed off each other, making an aggressive enough combination that it will also break down the bones rapidly. The goal is for an entire body to be broken down within 3 years, so potentially, every grave for whole body natural burial could be reused every 3-5 years. They are also intending to create a pod which will do this process above ground, eliminating issues of space.

This is a disruptive technology in so far as it challenges the shades of green – Bob feels he is working on defining what is considered green at the moment. Let Your Love Grow is getting world recognition now and their scientists are continuing research in the hope to dispel the myths around how we dispose of our loved ones and what is really green.

What is known is that his process is providing a therapeutic benefit for the grief and bereavement outcomes of the people who chose to use it.

Let your Love Grow logo – Image courtesy Bob Jenkins

THE DEATH DECK
LORI LOCICERO – CALIFORNIA, USA
https://thedeathdeck.com/

The Death Deck is a card game, designed to be used in a fun way to encourage conversation and ultimately increase a person's death literacy. It exists as a disruption to the conventional ways we talk about and engage with death in our society.

There are a few different decks of cards on the market which look to achieve a similar purpose as The Death Deck, such as Go Wish and The Conversation Game, but The Death Deck stands out because it is not just focused on end-of-life planning and decisions, it covers a broad set of areas in end-of-life literacy and encourages equally broad thinking. Ultimately, it asks people to determine what matters to them.

The idea for The Death Deck came out of the experience Lori had when her husband was diagnosed with cancer, and the events in the months that followed. When he was dying, they found that there was so much new and unexpected information, so many choices about things Lori wished she had known long before he took ill. Her husband had pancreatic cancer for a year, and they resisted hospice and palliative care until the end, because there was not enough knowledge or conversation about what it was and the benefits it could bring. The doctors spoke little of the possibility of death so they remained uneducated on many end-of-life issues.

Lori felt there was a need to uncover and unpack this experience for people and encourage honest conversations that extend the opportunity for people to get to know more about the end-of-life experience. In addition to that knowledge, she wanted to skill people to a point where they were able to simply be present with their loved one during that time rather than feel lost and distracted by all the chaotic learning that is usually required when someone is dying.

Co-creator of The Death Deck is Lisa, a hospice worker who came into their lives towards the end to help care for Lori's husband. Lori and Lisa connected and created a lovely bond which as the time went on became a friendship. Eventually, as her aftercare work with Lori ended, Lisa no longer visited and the connection drifted. When Lori started writing a memoir about her experiences through this journey she was prompted to reach out to Lisa for more details about the care her husband received. They reconnected as friends and eventually found themselves talking about a need to get other people talking before they needed to – an icebreaker of sorts – a light-hearted tool to normalise death and get people thinking about it as a part of life.

When they were testing out the name, they got pushback about using the word 'death' in the title. People were hesitant with the word but as creators, Lori and Lisa felt it was important to use it none the less; they were working on the premise that using the word helps to normalise the concept and incorporate it into life. The cards of The Death Deck are playful in their approach and cover various topics, infused with humour. The hope is that it will help people live better.

Lori likes to get groups of 6–10 people together to play: dinner and a game of cards. It is social learning and community capacity building rolled into one. Lori has noticed that it takes a little time for people to get comfortable with talking about the topics the cards bring up, but eventually people open up and it often becomes hard for the conversations to stop. It is not uncommon for the conversations to continue so intensely, that the game comes to a halt.

September 2021 was their three-year anniversary. They have had a successful beginning and are working on a model of community outreach and engagement. Theirs is a non-denominational game but they are open to variations. A modern Jewish group called 'Reboot' have asked her about a collaboration that they may be able to try to modernise and engage their younger communities. In this light they are also considering other types of themed decks.

From top: A wall of bones, Brno Ossuary, Brno, Czech Republic

A public *ofrenda* dedicated to deceased artists in the city of Oaxaca, Mexico

PART 3

ALTERNATIVE APPROACHES

It is worth noting that by alternative approaches, I am not referring to anything that could be construed as unconventional, hippy, ethically questionable or otherwise strange and unusual. Alternative approaches are alternatives to the contemporary methods of death and funeral care. Alternatives to current social convention. They embody new and old approaches to contemporary death practices.

GREENWOOD FUNERALS
PETER MACFADYEN, FROME UK
https://www.greenwoodfuneralhomes.com/
https://www.gosimplyfunerals.co.uk/

Peter Macfadyen wears many hats. He is one of the dedicated folks who are responsible for the reclaiming of the Frome Town Council and is the author of 'Flatpack Democracy' (both a book and model of governance). He is also the founder of Greenwood Funerals.

Peter and his colleagues at Greenwood Funerals run a business model where they do not mark up things like coffins, instead they charge for their time as a professional fee and the other things are at cost. Greenwood funerals organise cremations and coffins, ceremony and everything in between from the very simple to the very outlandish. The cost of cremations in the UK is approximately UK£700.00 (AUS$1,300.00) which is relatively expensive as a process, however coffins without the mark-ups are about UK£250.00 (AUS$470.00), making them more affordable than in Australia.

When arranging a funeral, Peter can visit the home of the family 3–4 times for planning, working closely with them to make sure things are exactly as the family want them. This is a vastly different approach to the contemporary industry model in the UK.

Peter's colleague has a fridge in her garage for those families who do not want the person's body kept at home. Greenwood offer transport for the deceased and work to educate their community about the options around dying and death. They have been operating since 2013 and do about 20 funerals a year.

One of the people who works with Greenwood is Angela, who has now also set up a service called Go Simply. Her business does about 10 funerals a week. They tend to be true to their name – simple and affordable offerings, although they do offer full-service packages as well. They have a similar transparent pricing system and do not mark up the optional extras. At the time of our interview, they also held the contract for the removal of bodies as required by the local police.

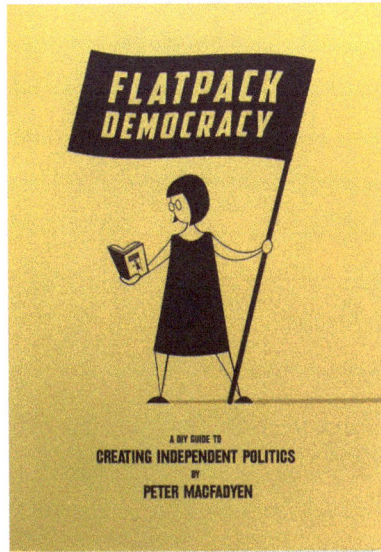

The cover of *Flatpack Democracy*, written by Peter McFadyen

The Greenwood funeral model needs to be seen in the light of the community it serves. Frome is a community with incredible capacity for people looking after people, and Peter has been instrumental in many of the changes in Frome. Politically, as a Councillor, he worked with the Independent for Frome Party to make decisions that were guided by the community and to instigate services for the community. Twenty-five percent of the Council's profit goes directly back into community projects and the Council, so dedicated to community initiatives, has an employee whose role is to increase the capacity of little groups and organisations. That role also helps to start new community-driven projects.

Frome does remarkably well at looking after their older residents as well. They have had a huge success with the implementation of the Compassionate Communities model of care movement which looks at community and end-of-life care, and theirs is the gold standard that others around the world aspire to (see Frome, in Part 4 for more details).

All this incredible capacity building happening in Frome has not translated into good death-care. After-death is a different and more familiar story for the residents of Frome and there remains a big gap in care and service provision. Even with services like Greenwood Funerals being readily accessible to the public, Peter finds people often will not go down the path of something 'new' when the time comes. This is not helped by the funeral industry there, where the care homes (similar to what is known as a nursing home in Australia) have contracts with mainstream funeral directors who do the 'removals' of people when they die. If the family is not happy with who has often already taken possession of their person's body, they can then nominate a different director, but often do not since this would involve having their person shunted around.

I asked Peter about how we could go about bridging this gap in community, about building more community capacity into the end-of-life and death care process, especially with a view to turn around the disempowerment that is occurring in death and hand it back to the families and communities.

Peter says we are up against a relatively new but intense taboo of death, the fear about the end of life, which in just 100 years has embedded deep in the western psyche – it is by taking this conversation public that we can start to address it. Through the festivals (like their very first Pushing Up the Daisies festival), death cafés, public education and community engagement – all of the things that create the safe space for people to think about, talk about and engage with death – we can begin to peel back those layers of fear and work towards increasing death literacy and community capacity at the end of life. This has the added bonus of changing how grief and bereavement are experienced in the western world as well.

ONLY WITH LOVE

CLAIRE TURNHAM MBE – UK AND NEW ZEALAND

https://www.onlywithlove.co.uk/

The best person to care for a loved one is a loved one[4]

Claire Turnham

Claire started Only With Love in 2014. It is a family-led funeral service and the aim is to empower, enable and educate families and communities to care for their own. She came to death through a realisation she had when her dad died: it dawned on her that as a group, they were the best people to care for her dad in life and they were still the best people to care for him in death.

She wanted others to have this experience as well. To this end she holds 'gentle death' workshops for various communities along with a death care service for family and community. Her role is to be flexible and meet the family where they are, with whatever needs they have.

Only With Love operates on a unique business model that embodies ideas of equity and social justice. Claire does not charge for her time. Instead, she gives each family the same service, regardless of their ability to pay. At the beginning of her work with a family she tells them that at the end of her work with them she will let them know how many hours she has spent in their service and they are welcome to pay what they feel is fair and affordable for them. Doing this, Claire feels that she gives a valuable and meaningful service every time and she feels as though she has been paid far more than she ever would have charged.

Claire spends a lot of time on the details, including crafting the ceremony. She is happy to work with families who want home funerals or blended services (with or without a funeral director), she will mentor the family with the body care beforehand, and help with any other requirements they may have, including body transport. Where the family do not want to do body care at home, or where it is not possible, she will help make it happen for them at the funeral home.

Claire believes that funerals and death care belong with the families. To this end she provides families with the equipment and information to do exactly as they wish. According to Claire, home funerals are a healing experience where a family can step into their own power. She only works with one family at a time and only once since 2014 has she had to turn a family away as she was not physically present to support them. In that case she had been working with them for about 18 months prior to the death and when the death came the family were so empowered that they did not need her.

Claire builds friendships because of the close bonds that are formed through the service she gives. She stays in contact with her people and they, her. There is none of the distance found commonly in the industry once a funeral is complete. She does community talks with attendance of up to 100 people at a time and she holds varying workshops. Wherever she is asked to go, if it is possible, she does, and this includes overseas. More recently she has relocated to New Zealand where she continues to work, teach and educate in communities as well as in hospice facilities.

While living in the UK, Claire set up the UK Home Funeral Network. She continues to be Chair of that organisation. Many of the independent funeral businesses that have started in the UK have come from the training she provides. Claire says that families in the UK are in a unique position, as there are very few rules and regulations governing what can and cannot be done by way of a home funeral. The only requirements are that the death must be registered within 5 days and that the body, when being transported on a public road, must be covered. This affords family freedoms that do not exist elsewhere. Natural burial in the UK has also been hugely popular, and this goes hand in hand with home funerals – the two are starting to merge into a symbiotic relationship.

For those who cannot afford funeral services – and there are a growing number of people in this position – Only With Love offers a 'suspended coffin service', where people can purchase a coffin from her and 'pay it forward' to other families who may not have been able to afford it themselves. This grass roots movement towards home-based death care is a process of reclaiming.

Claire believes that we need more networking, more collaboration, joining and extending our services to each other – supporting each other. As medical services, funeral directors, doulas and home funeral guides we need to walk hand in hand to grow. Public education is key for Claire. Doctors, hospice workers, nurses as well as the general public need to know what all the options are, so that together they can work towards better experiences for the clients and communities.

Claire Turnham and Jerrigrace Lyons instructing on the body care of a deceased at the 2019 Nation Home Funeral Alliance Conference, Minnesota USA

As a celebrant, Claire can be engaged by both clients and the funeral industry to be the celebrant in funeral services. Her entire workload is dependent on word of mouth and referral, she does no formal advertising. When working in New Zealand, this is particularly important as ceremony is the integral component of after-death care and ritual and people will often go to the celebrant before they go to the funeral director.

Claire feels that we need to be careful about how we frame our conversations with families. Families and communities need to remain at the centre of the care, no matter whether they have used a funeral director or not. Like many others, Claire highlights a responsibility to stay away from language defined by the contemporary industry. For example, people often talk about what the funeral directors will and will not allow a family to do. Claire's focus is different; it is not up to her to allow anything. Families need to know what their rights are when it comes to their deceased person and further, they need to know that they own those rights before they can choose to give them away.

She finds the bond between people who take this approach to death care together does not go away, and she includes herself in that, as the people she helps stay connected with her. This approach to the end of life is enhancing the positive grief and bereavement outcomes for everyone involved. Everything she does is done only with love; she goes into the family with no expectations. Her focus is always on the family maintaining the agency and space to grow into their grief their own way.

Claire is turning convention on its head. She is another rebel in the system, running a successful practice with no set fees. She creates personal and unique experiences while letting people know where they can save money. Claire feels as though her services get better with time. Families appreciate what she does for them at the time of death but it is with the passage of time that they begin to fully appreciate the gravity and the benefit of having had her work with them.

Claire sees that as an alternative approach, Only With Love should not be about training more people and offering a new version of 'funeral'. It is about teaching and empowering families so that they do not need her at all; families finding the capacity to look after their own. When given the right skills and knowledge, families can make choices that reflect the person. Authenticity and the space to express it is integral to the home funeral process.

This is a disruptive alternate approach, building better grief and bereavement outcomes for families, but for Claire it is also a way of life – she home birthed, home schooled, and now home death cares.

OSCAR FREDRIK AND WAHLS

RASMUS RINGBORG,
GOTHENBURG SWEDEN
https://www.momentobyraerna.se/ofw/

Sweden is an interesting place with a very different approach to funerals – there it is a government concern. Everyone is entitled to a funeral to the extent that official contributions are made from both the church and/or the government.

In Gothenburg I met with Rasmus Ringborg, a funeral director from Oscar Fredrik & Wahls. This is one of a large chain, that in total own 28 percent of the market and about 200+ funeral homes. Their parent company is called Fonus.

When Rasmus started directing, it was customary to wait up to 60 days between death and burial or cremation. Over time legislation has changed to reduce the time to a maximum of only 30 days. This has been a huge cultural shift in thinking. As a result, more people now have a cremation first (within the 30 days) and a ceremony later because they feel it is too rushed for them to have the funeral within 30 days. For those who do stick to that time frame, they wait as long as possible (25–30 days) for the funeral. Rasmus feels that it is good for families to have this time to think and plan rather than rush.

The process there when a person dies is also different to what some in the West have come to expect. In Sweden bodies are transported from the place of death immediately to the hospital and this is the case for everyone, regardless of the funeral director chosen. It is a designated transport company who does that, and families are not charged for this service – it is provided by the government.

In Gothenburg there are two hospitals that provide the refrigeration for all funeral homes, and each can store over 70 bodies. Once it is time to prepare the body the transport people collect and prepare the deceased with the clothes provided by the family, then they encoffin the body and take it to a *bisattninglokal* which literally translates to 'corpse house'. These are communal facilities located inside cemeteries and bodies can stay here for weeks.

Entrance to the Haga District, Gothenburg, Sweden

Rasmus says that funeral directors are not too involved in the practices around preparation of the body, and neither are the families. In fact, viewings are not too common. Interestingly, in Stockholm it is standard practice to embalm everyone, while in Gothenburg it is not, although the processes are the same otherwise and he puts this down to regional differences. The exception to this is when someone dies at home. Then, his transport people, if the family request, can arrive at the family home with a coffin and dress the person and put them in the coffin there. The families are not involved in this, but they are allowed to witness it and the body is then taken straight to the *bisattninglokal*.

In Gothenburg the vast majority of people are cremated. This is not cost driven, since burials and cremations cost about the same. Rasmus considers that it is just their way. There are a lot of cemeteries around there though and he did say that space is becoming premium. You can fit four coffins into a grave (2mx2m), or 36 urns.

With the (long) wait times between death and ceremony comes much more detailed planning and the families tend to touch base with the directors regularly. They have a range of different clients from time to time, from those who want to engage with every minute detail of planning and preparation over the 30 days to others who leave it largely up to the directors.

In Sweden they use officiants or priests depending on family preference; in a country of 10.2 million people just over 57 percent of them are still members of a church, even though many of them are no longer religious. Celebrants are free: they are provided by the municipality, but it is also possible to contract the services of a specific celebrant of choice, where they get paid the rough equivalent of AUD$400.00.

Every family gets a hardcover memorial book for free after the service. The book includes pictures of the newspaper notices, the order of service, any cards or wishes sent, and about 50 photos from the funeral service.

There is a big environmental focus in Sweden, right down to the fuel used in their vehicles, which is apparently more environmentally friendly. There are two coffin factories which supply coffins for all the funeral homes – both factories are in Falkoping and both offer environmentally friendly options – one even uses the heat from the coffin production to heat the factory.

Funerals in Sweden cost between the equivalent of AUD$2,000.00 and AUD$27,000.00 with the average being approximately AUD$6,500.00. Every adult, working or not, pays an annual 'funeral fee' to the government – much like a tax system. This is about AUD$30.00 and covers at least the transport from the church or chapel to the cemetery or crematorium. The family pay for the transfers from the 'corpse house' to the church/place of ceremony (if the ceremony is not held in the cemetery where the body is stored); they also pay for the transport from the hospital to the *bisattninglokal*.

Funeral poverty as a concept is less of a problem in Sweden since their basic costs are low and the government maintains a stance that everybody is entitled to a funeral. To this end, if an estate is worth less than AUD$3,000.00 the municipality will pay the difference in funeral costs up to that amount.

Home Funerals are a long way from being viable in Sweden as the customs around the extended time from death to ceremony is entrenched in their society, and further, there is not the drive to ease the financial burden of funerals as they are contributed to so readily by government.

VILA BEGRAVNING FUNERAL CEREMONY

JENNY-ANN GUNNARSSON – GOTHENBURG, SWEDEN

http://vilabegravning.se/

Jenny-Ann is an independent funeral director and Sweden's first end-of-life doula. Family-led funerals have not really come to Sweden, but as an independent, Jenny-Ann works with families and encourages them to do things themselves any way they can. Her motivation for doing this is both for cost and for the benefits she knows there to be in relation to grieving. In Sweden, Jenny-Ann told me, it is possible for a family to buy a coffin from a funeral director, pick up the body from the morgue and transport the body themselves, but it is rarely done.

Financial considerations are rarely a concern among the mainstream society. Because of the government contribution, families are able to simply work within the budget of what they know will come to them for the funeral costs. If the person who has died is a member of the Swedish Church, the Church contributes financially, provides the venue, the musician, and the minister at no extra charge. There is, however, an ongoing cost to church membership. If a person has church membership that has lapsed, to be entitled to any benefit they would need to re-join the church, which can be quite expensive.

In the bigger cities, it is often the case that upon death, a body will be taken to a hospital morgue and then the chosen funeral director takes over. In this case, the family gets to take the time they need before making any decisions, like choosing a coffin. Family are able to attend the hospital to help dress their person; they can have a small viewing or ceremony there as well. Once the body has been prepared, arrangements are made for the funeral home to take the body to the *bisattninglokal*.

In the case of a death at home, a family may request that the funeral directors come to the home with a coffin and prepare the body there. This bypasses the need to use the hospital mortuary. If this is the case the funeral directors deliver the body straight to the *bisattninglokal*. There are several of these

bisattninglokal in the chapels or crematoria around Sweden. This is also where the secular services can be held, at no cost for the venue.

Jenny-Ann attends the morgue and does the washing and dressing of the deceased body once she has arranged and organised the funeral with the family. Families can accompany her to the hospital morgue if they wish. It is not standard practice to wash every body, only as needed or if the family have requested it. It is not routine to use makeup or do cosmetic procedures on a body either.

Jenny-Ann meets with each family after the funeral to debrief with them and give them the memorial book she puts together. They can talk about the service and process, then have the opportunity to provide feedback and she gives them a gift which is usually the candle holder that was used for the service.

While the funeral industry does have regulation in Sweden, licensing is not required for the role of funeral director. Jenny-Ann trained just outside of Stockholm before she started her own business and she was clear from the start that she wanted her focus to be entirely on the experience of the family. While she has met with some opposition in the industry, she continues with her vision – to provide a holistic service to the families, doing as much of it as she is asked and encouraging their input and contributions.

As a small business owner, Jenny-Ann does a lot herself. She has been running this business for over six years and averages 3–4 funerals a month. She has no intention of becoming a big company. She cares for the bodies, does the paperwork, the funeral directing and arranging. There is a grief counsellor and a lawyer who work with her when people need those services, she has casuals to call on if a service is expected to have over 60 people. Her husband does the books and administration, and she has someone who assists with her transport. In Sweden the independent directors have their own little network and often help each other – the bigger homes do not work with them.

Working as a funeral director has always been work Jenny-Ann enjoys, although she is now finding herself increasingly drawn to the role of a death doula, which until recently she never knew that such a thing existed. She nursed her mum through the last 6 weeks of her life – her mum died at home with her family around her, and while it was not planned, it was a beautiful experience for them all.

Jenny-Ann reflected on the experience, describing it as being *'high on death'*. She said that the experience was so intimate, honest, intense and rewarding. She wanted to do more with this experience and so she went to talk to the funeral director who helped with her mum's funeral and her career took off from there. As a part of her business she works with people who are pre-planning their deaths and now she wants to extend a doula-style service to them as well.

Jenny-Ann is not sure where Sweden's tradition of 60 days from death to ceremony came from. In the old days, people would die at home, be cared for at home and leave from there to burial. She remembers people would talk about storing wood for a coffin in the attic of their homes and eventually they would make their own coffins. When someone died there would be a large wake and the body would be cared for at home. It was traditional to arrange pine branches around the coffin to help with the odour (they did not have modern methods of cooling), and pine branches would be laid at the front of churches with the tips turned a certain direction. This was believed to help the deceased person's journey of moving on.

By comparison, Jenny-Ann says her funerals these days are quite small, certainly smaller than in other countries. The now 30-day time frame between death and ceremony is used to grieve and to plan – it is considered a quiet time for moving into grief. Two weeks is the shortest turnaround she has ever had, most people preferring to take as much time as they can. The 30-day rule exists for the body disposal, not the ceremony, but people will usually have a ceremony in that time.

If a person is cremated in Sweden the ashes must stay in the crematorium until it is decided what will happen to them. After death, the body and the ashes belong to the state so as a funeral director, Jenny-Ann can collect the urn and keep it for a little while if she is to bring the ashes to a ceremony. As a private citizen, no one is allowed to collect the ashes, keep them at home, or separate them. If a family collect the ashes they must have arranged a placement for them prior to their collection.

The only way to be able to have ashes at home for a time in Sweden is to seek permission to scatter them, and then only scattering over water; land scattering is very rare. If that permission is granted, the authorities will produce the required permit for the funeral director or crematorium to release the ashes. When scattering, there are strict guidelines: the family have to declare where and which month a scattering is to happen, show the place on a map, and in the case of scattering on the water, it has to be 100m out from land.

Upon collection, a family need to show the permission to scatter and their ID before they will be handed the ashes. There is a piece of paper that accompanies the ashes, which is a declaration that needs to be sworn upon the scattering taking place, stating that the ashes were scattered as per the permission granted. No one audits these or checks up on these in practice, but it is certainly presented as quite a strict system. This process is the only way for a family to be able to access the ashes and do what they want with them

There seems to be a real fear around the protection of remains. To split ashes into portions is considered to be disrespectful to the deceased. Jenny-Ann has no idea where this protectionist attitude has come from. There is an idea of contamination around bodies, some people go so far as to believe that if a family rent a coffin and put the urn of ashes in it for the ceremony (which is not unusual when a ceremony is held more than 30 days after death) they say that coffin cannot be used again. Social convention dictates that it should be destroyed.

Because of the Swedish system and governance, everyone is looked after and so there is less formal paperwork around dying, such as the Australian Enduring Guardian and Power of Attorney. Jenny-Ann has developed a wishes and planning document that talks about the before and after-death wishes for the families to use as a guide. People still use Wills, but the other documents we talk about as vital in Australia are not considered as intrinsic in Sweden's culture. In Sweden, a person's input to their Will is somewhat limited, they can only decide on what will happen to half of the estate's value, the other half automatically goes to the Next of Kin (if you are married that is your spouse, otherwise to children etc.). It is not a dissimilar idea in Australia, where a basic goal of our law in estate planning is that a person must provide for their family – this is often a basis upon which Wills can be contested, but our law does not specify amounts.

The communities here in Sweden are slowly building their death literacy but only in the context of their conventional system. This means that people are willing to talk more about death as an abstract subject, but less about their own mortality. There is a real lack of knowledge in the community of what the process is when someone dies – where the bodies are kept, how they are dealt with, etc. In addition to a lack of knowledge, there is a level of chosen ignorance. Jenny-Ann has observed that people only want to know about the pretty things or the gory things about death, not the realities. She also sees language as adding to this. In Sweden when it comes to death they say, *'I'm sorry for your grief'*, making grief regrettable and stigmatising it in people's minds, rather than normalise it as a part of life.

The grief and bereavement outcomes for the Swedish in their current end-of-life and death care practices have much room for improvement. Even with the longer time given to plan, the 'on the ground' outcomes are not entirely healthy overall. People lead busy lives. Those who are working might take a few days off but then go back to work and often find that the social supports are not there – people do not want to talk about death so the bereaved have no one to talk to.

Then when the funeral is done the attitude is that the grieving must be finished – people start to be surprised if friends and colleagues are still grieving after six months. Crying in public is not encouraged and it is often met with the attitude of needing to make excuses for it or encouraging people to be strong. The grieving person seems to be required to appear apologetic for making others uncomfortable by displaying their grief.

Jenny-Ann often has the bereaved say to her that their grieving does not really start properly until the funeral is done and at that time, the social supports are not there. While finance is much less of a concern here, the lack of community capacity still makes it very difficult for people and this is something she hopes to address through the growth of the doula role.

NATIONAL END OF LIFE DOULA ASSOCIATION, GREEN BURIAL COUNCIL, NATIONAL HOME FUNERAL ALLIANCE

LEE WEBSTER – USA

https://www.homefuneralalliance.org/
https://www.nedalliance.org/
https://www.greenburialcouncil.org/

Lee Webster is one of the founding people of the entire end-of-life grass roots movement in the USA and her contributions have been far too many to list. She sees her role as a connector between the people in all of these spaces.

America is further along than both Australia and the UK in relation to the organisation and formation of peak bodies in this space. Lee had been instrumental in this development from the start, being involved in the creation of many of the member organisations which are now providing strong leadership in the reclaiming of end-of-life and after-death care.

These organisations have members around the world, and they build systems of support and communication between practitioners. They are providing resources and education as well as empowerment while seeking to put a uniform structure into what has been an organically grown grassroots movement. We are now at a point where there needs to be a clearly defined scope of what the roles of each service provider are, what they offer and how they are going to present and manage those services going forward.

In relation to doulas, because the role is largely undefined at the moment, there is concern that some doulas may be overstepping by doing things such as body care and transport of the deceased. Doulas want to be considered professionals, and many of them are increasingly going into business offering this service as their profession.

Practitioners need to be mindful that there are social justice issues around creating an essentially narrow, white middle-class service that is just something else that families have to find money to pay for. Without due consideration and a carefully planned approach, there is a real risk of excluding both the marginalised communities and the many family groups who may want to do this for themselves, but do not know how to advocate for themselves to make it happen.

Because of the blurring that has at times occurred between the roles of home funeral guide and doula in the USA, the outcome has at times been that doulas are doing the work of the home funeral guides, which in and of itself is not a problem if they have the knowledge to do so. The problem is that they are also at times going further, not only providing support and guidance to families who are caring for their dead, but by actually performing the work themselves, providing transport or body care for a deceased.

The role of a doula ends at the point of death. While a doula can be engaged by either the person dying, their family or both, they are generally a non-medical support for the person who is dying and their family. After death the family may choose to keep the doula on as a guide and a support, especially if they have chosen a home funeral for their person, but the doula's role does not extend to taking possession of the body of the deceased, transporting, washing, dressing or otherwise caring for the dead. That role belongs to the family alone.

The doula role is coming on so fast and it has been largely unchecked until now. Many who have been doing this work for decades see that there is a growing risk of something going very wrong with a practitioner who was not adequately trained at handling a body. If that were to happen, the entire movement could be set back or shut down out of fear and a lack of understanding.

Lee Webster has spoken to many doula trainers and not many of them are aware of the difference between the after-death and before-death care and where the lines are between the two. We need to define the roles and work within the guidelines in order to build the legitimacy in the role from a public perception standpoint.

Doulas have been unregulated until recently and there is a need to bring them together. To this end the National End of Life Doula Alliance was created in the USA. NEDA started in about 2018, as a way to bring doulas together and start looking at frameworks of support, guidance, networking and education around doulas and their services.

Lee approached NEDA saying that she had developed a model for building a level of accountability into the space. Using a proficiency based approach, they have introduced a proficiency exam as a form of micro-credentialing. The credentialing is not equivalent to an industry certification. There is no entity willing to hold the liability for certification; it is simply too cost prohibitive and there would need to be further regulations before this could happen. If there was a certifying body, then it would be responsible for the actions of the certified persons. Instead, micro-credentialing is a middle ground and a good first step.

This system of proficiency offers a badge for the successful practitioner, that can be used in marketing a service. Along with the level of confidence a proficiency badge brings to the public, micro-credentialing is also a way to bring accountability to trainers.

No course provider can afford to teach a course that does not leave their student with the knowledge to pass a proficiency exam. This is also a way to get the many and varied people providing training in this doula space to be on the same page, teaching the same core concepts. The result is that across the board, there can be a level of confidence in the skill and knowledge of any proficient service provider a person chooses to hire, regardless of where they received their training.

The National Home Funeral Alliance started out as a professional organisation but soon realised that as an operating model, it was not sustainable. Home funeral guides offer a different service to funeral directors and there is already a funeral industry. If home funeral guides want to do the work of funeral directors they need to get a licence and join that industry. There is a perception that all home funeral guides are nicer and cheaper than funeral directors which is not always the case – 'cheaper' is also not the only point of home funerals.

When working as a funeral guide, Lee does not go on site with a family when they are caring for their dead. She gives support and education to the families before the death and is available to them by phone if they need it after – so families can do things themselves and there is no detraction or distraction from them as a family and community group doing the work to care for their person. She is not the authority in the room for them because, if properly supported, the only authority they need is their own.

Providing death care to their people themselves is actively building the families' skills, death literacy levels and also the community capacity for the people around them. Lee believes that if a family needs hand-holding through the process, then they need some form of licensed professional with them. A home funeral guide or a doula is not equipped, licensed or in many cases appropriately trained to be hands-on with the body of a deceased person. The point of home funerals is the family doing it themselves. Home funeral guides and doulas are not the after-death body care professionals.

Most families Lee has worked with prefer a blended style of care where they keep the body for a day or two and then work with a contemporary funeral director of some kind. Families like the option of a gentler letting go and giving after-death care themselves but prefer not to do everything else (such as paperwork, registrations). This is one of the reasons Lee feels like we need to be walking more the middle ground, and as far as possible working with the contemporary industry. We need to be respecting the place that the funeral directors have and what they offer. If a family make an informed choice to engage a contemporary funeral director, this is just as valid a choice as if they had chosen a complete family-led home funeral.

Lee wrote for and compiled a book entitled 'Changing Landscapes', a textbook for a course that only started to be taught in mortuary schools in America a few years ago. They are well into the teaching of it now, and what this means is that the new generation of funeral directors are coming through with more knowledge and an open mind to the other options available for death care.

They are better skilled in the knowledge of the rights of the family and are able to provide a wider set of choices and options. This is about change from within. We do not need another layer of professionals. We need a skilled public and an educated and willing industry that are open to the public knowing that they can, and knowing how, to look after their own.

The Green Burial Council holds a credentialing standard for their burial grounds. If you are going to be credentialed for doing this work, you need to know what you are doing. If you are going to be approved by the Green Burial Council, you have to be doing things right.

The Green Burial Council was the first of the three movements to build this kind of legitimacy for their members. They developed a system of proficiency for the Green Burial Grounds that needed to be proven before the Council will endorse their practices as green. This has not been without its difficulty, but it is now a well-accepted and established model in relation to accountability in this space.

The Green Burial Council has expanded in recent years to endorse not only burial grounds but also certain products as well. All of this is designed to educate the public, assist them with options and inform the conversations people are having with service providers.

All of these organisations and structures, the Green Burial Council, National Home Funeral Alliance and National End of Life Doula Alliance, are completely voluntary. People get involved, serve on boards and committees, dedicate countless hours in their busy lives and they are doing it because they believe in it wholeheartedly.

Only recently have they started to see much needed new blood come through, and with that come fresh ideas and directions. Lee knows how much more work there is to do. While her contributions have been enormous, there is a long road ahead. With the introduction of standards and proficiency, it is hoped that public confidence and awareness will grow and these groups will continue to thrive.

First meeting of the Los Angeles Doula Collective hosted by Birgitta Katsenbaum, Los Angeles, California, USA

LA DOULA COLLECTIVE
BIRGITTA KATSENBAUM
https://bridgingtransitions.net/

I attended the first of the LA Doula Collective gatherings, hosted by Birgitta Katsenbaum. The idea was to bring doulas together to share ideas and provide a network of understanding and support for one another. So many end-of-life practitioners do their work solo and spending time with other similar minded people can be enriching. There were so many women who turned up that day from different parts of Los Angeles and it was an eclectic mix of nineteen people who shared the same drive to serve others. I was able to make connections there and I interviewed some of them individually.

I met with many wonderful women and what struck me was the wealth of knowledge and experience that gathered in that room. Some of them did not know each other and for many this was a first meeting. It was a reminder about how grassroots movements form, how with one small gesture a network is born and how some surprising things come from the most chance meetings.

The afternoon was one of valuable connection and it was important because what I witnessed was a coming together of like minds to share information, receive support and encouragement and brainstorm about what they can do together. It was the birth of what I hope becomes a force for change in their local communities, addressing the fragmentation which is all too common when movements grow quickly. This is capacity building in action.

Discussions around fellowships, creating collaborations and ways to engage with communities and services to enhance the end-of-life experiences for the dying and their families made for a meeting of the minds which has an incredible potential and I look forward to seeing what blooms from here. You will find reports on my interviews with some of these people throughout this publication.

Funeral directors, home funeral guides, doulas, social workers, trainers and many others spent the afternoon openly sharing their work, ideas and what I found was a fantastic example of the community networks we need here in Australia – this kind of network has the potential for real, large scale community change.

FRIENDS ALTERNATIVE FUNERAL HOME
ZIRI RIDEAUX – CALIFORNIA, USA
https://friendsfs.ca/

Based in Venice Beach, Ziri is a death midwife and funeral director. Her funeral service is wide ranging, from those who want big and elaborate services to those who are out on the weekends washing cars on the side of the road to pay for them. She keeps overheads as small as possible and works out of her home as a way to keep costs to a minimum. Her business serves 15–20 cases a month.

Ziri has provided a funeral for a biker, a Viking funeral and a few surfer funerals as well as many other memorial style events. Ziri works with people before or after death. Her focus is more holistic than the mainstream industry. She does as much as possible to honour the wishes of the dying and the dead. For example she has taken people before they died to the forest to spend time there if they have wanted to die in nature.

Ziri is keenly aware of all of the legislative requirements in her state and is able to work with families to make people's choices their reality. All of this takes intricate planning, and to this end she has developed a 12-page Advance Care Directive document in conjunction with hospice workers and lawyers, which allows people to document the full range of options and choices for the end of life.

Death has always been a part of Ziri's life, since the age of four. She was trained by her great-grandmother and grandmother, who were practitioners of the Siberian traditions, to sit bedside and work with the dying. It is a legacy of wisdom from generations of women that she carries with her. Ziri had gone on as an adult to work in several war-torn countries as a war correspondent and upon returning, she volunteered in a funeral home before deciding to start her own business approximately ten years ago. She went on to become licensed as a funeral director in order to be able to fully serve the families the way that she wanted to.

Her work with families is as 'hands-on' or 'hands off' as required. The process around death regarding the legalities and paperwork, has become very complicated and while a family can do things for themselves, it is often hard for them. Ziri believes that our ways of death and dying have been kidnapped for profit and we need to reclaim them and re-humanise death for families.

She encourages the families to order their own coffins and urns etc. to save on cost, and she charges for everything she provides, including her time. There are additional costs for things such as embalming if needed, but she is able to lower her personal charge to compensate.

Ziri's parents were from Romania, a Communist country, and while she was born in Germany they brought her up with their Romanian influence and she carries this with her still. She is always trying to find a fair financial balance, to be able to pay people fairly for their work with her and not overcharge customers. She has a small core staff and casuals she can call on, and shares some of her staff with other funeral homes, such as drivers etc. She works with crematorium staff who can do body preparations for her. Ziri also uses a centralised crematorium who can do transport, body storage and preparation. She has agreements with these facilities all over the city so that she can offer her services right throughout Los Angeles.

The difference with the holistic approach Ziri offers, is that it holds at its core the mentality that the families remain the sole focus, there is no corporatisation about it. Ziri approaches the families she serves as her friends, hence the name she has given her business. She feels that doing funerals this way allows families to more authentically step into their own grief.

People tend to shut down when pain starts, she explained, and the funeral industry has ways of encouraging this. The holistic process is about surrendering to the pain and in return experiencing emotional growth and learning. Ziri sees this process as similar to that of birth – if you shut down and tense up in childbirth the baby doesn't come, you need to relax into the pain for it to flow. It is the same with death: you will be forever changed, you will grow and potentially have more of a compassionate outlook moving forward.

Death changes people. Ziri helps people to accept this process and holds the space for it to change them, allowing people to remain in control of the process but also to be vulnerable and ask for help. Ziri sees family centred death care as the dying person's great gift to those they will leave behind, a gift of the remarkable opportunity to experience the kind of growth that comes from death. She has travelled to many parts of the world and found that in the shamanic traditions of many different countries, the connections and gifts at the end of life are treated with a certain similar reverence and there is an underlying truth to the experience which is centred on growth.

Friends Alternative Funeral Home will work with any and all religions – in all cases, she works with families on their own terms. She has even done ceremonies for people as do-overs (re-doing or replicating a ceremony that has been done before), forgiveness ceremonies and the like for unresolved emotions. People come to her looking for closure on situations or relationships and for continuity, so that people can find their own way of holding the dead in their lives going forward.

Ziri runs a simple accounting system and looks after her own accounts but is currently investigating ways of making her funeral home a not-for-profit entity. She is looking at different models and ways of ethically responding to the community, as well as a way of having this as a point of difference. She hopes a not-for-profit would allow her to serve families who do not have the financial capacity – currently she does this from her own pocket. As a not-for-profit it would be a more sustainable model to continue serving people based on equity and community need.

In Los Angeles, there is a huge community need. Despite the obvious affluence, in places there is an overwhelming poverty crisis. At present, if a homeless person dies and the family or friends have no money to pay for a funeral service or cremation, the county morgue will keep the body for three months before they cremate them and put the ashes into a mass grave. Ziri explained that the families of these dead are not entitled to get the ashes back after that three months – if the county pays for the cremation, the ashes all must go into mass graves. She considers it is a dehumanising process. It is hard to disagree.

Friends, as a business, does not advertise at all. Instead Ziri asks families to write her reviews online instead. She has done close to 3000 funerals in the last eight years. When she started it was 3–4 funerals a month maximum and it took a long time to establish and for people to know her and use her service. Word of mouth is important and so is public education. Ziri has spent a lot of time going to old age homes and libraries and is not scared to have the difficult conversations.

She feels this is key to the authentic connections she is making with people. Families know that her funeral home is an advocate for them. Ziri will work with people to help them make their choices and make sure their wishes are carried out at the time. She believes this is sacred, community based work. Funeral support, like education, should be a free, or at least affordable, service.

Ziri feels that it should be removed from the 'corporate business' model. One way to change this mindset would be to incorporate mandatory death care service just like mandatory military service. Young people could be given options – military, mental health, death etc. This would help increase people's community capacity and sense of social justice and would also build their death literacy from a young age.

Another service Ziri is providing when she works with a family (if they are open to it) is a 'meet the dead' experience where she brings an interested member of the public with her to interact with the dead, allowing people to break the taboos and confront their fears. She finds this encourages conversations and connections within the communities and as a by-product the entire experience is therapeutic and helpful for everyone.

Ziri believes that if people are no longer afraid of death, they can no longer be blackmailed into the hamster wheel of life and death. People can feel free to make choices and take risks without the fear of what will happen if we don't just earn money. It is a radical and bold approach, but what social change has ever begun without radical thinkers? Her goal is to take us from what we have become – a society with death approaches based on fear – to one where, by confronting and moving past those fears we find ourselves opened up and ultimately living better lives in service of each other.

CLARITY FUNERALS AND CREMATION
CAITLIN DOUGHTY – CALIFORNIA USA
https://www.clarityfunerals.com/

Known for so many things including her internet videos on Ask a Mortician and the social movement that is The Order of the Good Death, Caitlin is arguably the USA's most public figure in the advocacy space for doing death better. She is a staunch advocate for families – not the industry, the doulas or the alternate space, although many people working in those spaces closely identify with her. She believes in the value of a family interacting with their dead and she is now part of a new funeral service, Clarity, a green-focused, affordable funeral service.

Caitlin has built a brand around her education and advocacy and the benefit of this is that it provides her with an international platform to promote all the disruptions and differences she sees happening in the end-of-life space. Because her funding comes from the public through sites like Patreon, she is not pushing anyone's agenda but her own and Caitlin's focus is very much on advocacy for home funerals and for families being hands-on with the after-death body care of their person.

Grief and engagement with the body of a person after death are inextricably linked. There is a kind of incredible power to be found in the action of touch and the deliberate act of being present with the dead. Something very real and very beautiful happens to people who give care to their dead and that keeps her engaged and doing this work.

The contemporary approaches to funerals mean that we are largely missing the acceptance of death, along with the bravery that comes when a person makes the choice to witness the reality of a death and all that reality entails. Caitlin explained, when the body of a person is removed after death there is an expectation created that the family's only job is to have the feelings of grief – others will take care of everything. What that means in reality is that people are experiencing sadness and grief without ever having any real outlet, or framework, with which to experience those intense emotions. Caring for the body of their person is just one of many meaningful outlets. Washing and dressing the dead allows a family space and time to arrive at the place where they are ready to let go – this is the beginning of grief with agency.

There is another point about expectation – Caitlin pointed out that what is considered acceptable with a body when the family are giving care can be vastly different to what is acceptable when that body is in the care of 'professionals'. The industry goes to great lengths to show death to be beautiful, like someone is simply sleeping – when a family give the after-death care it has a much more raw element to it and they find, even unknowingly, that they have the capacity to see death for what it is, without the masks often used by the industry.

Something else that Caitlin believes completely is that there needs to be far less money in death. To this end she works to build community capacity, skilling people to care for their dead. She creates online videos and talks about the realities of death care to offer people a transparent look at how it works.

Caitlin would also like to see an online platform offering specific resources. She hopes it will include things like the step-by-step 'how to' processes of after-death care, state-based information on paperwork and regulations for things such as transport. She would like to see lists of funeral directors happy to work with families who want to have home death care and much more. As a holistic platform this has the potential to be a widespread vehicle for capacity building across America.

The concerns about end-of-life doulas are the same for Caitlin as they are for many in the USA. While the benefits of doulas in this space are well known, not only is there the risk of creating a service that excludes all those who cannot afford it – and some might argue that those vulnerable people who cannot afford it are the ones who need it the most – but there is also the issue of crossing the line between the work of a doula and a funeral director. Much of this comes from the fact that to date we have not been very good at defining the roles and the differences between them. This is something that we need to be much more proactive about. It is hoped that the micro-credentialing through peak bodies will also address this.

At present funeral directors require licensing for every aspect of the business. In many other countries this is unnecessary, including Australia. While Caitlin is a fan of bureaucratic credentialing for things such as inspection of environmental, sales, burial and cremation records she feels that the level of licensing required in America is over the top – it adds to the public's idea that they cannot provide their own after-death care, that they do in fact need a funeral director.

I asked Caitlin how she thinks we should be educating the funeral industry, how do we belay the fears that we are a threat? She has attended some of the big industry conferences and given presentations. In 2018 it was to a divided room where there were some visibly interested in her position and others not. Many funeral directors however are starting to realise that in order to maintain their own continued relevance in a changing market they need to stay current, and that includes opening up to changes that are happening socially around death. The directory that Caitlin envisages may also go some way to help with this.

When considering her own mortality, Caitlin says she would like to be wrapped in a simple shroud and buried in a grave that will be used again a few years from then. The re-use of graves is just one of the future directions she holds hope for, alkaline hydrolysis and human composting being among the others. Until then she will continue finding ways to take death to the mainstream with the hope to increase community capacity.

GOING WITH GRACE
ALUA ARTHUR – CALIFORNIA, USA
http://www.goingwithgrace.com/

Alua Arthur has one of the most public of profiles worldwide when it comes to the role of a doula and she is also a former board member of the National End of Life Doula Alliance.

Alua spends a great deal of her time educating the public and provides online training. Her training is designed to allow people to arrive at a very clear perspective of their own death and relationship to it. It is an approach to preparedness for one's own mortality and through this people have the opportunity to discover their own biases and explore what death means to them. It is not conventional doula training but there is quite an element of practical skill within it.

I asked Alua about the issues of inclusivity in the doula movement, having been at the National Home Funeral Alliance conference in 2019 where this was widely discussed as a problematic issue. Inclusivity has not been a problem in her experience. Being a woman of colour, she finds the people who come to her are from varied backgrounds and ethnicities and she is training people from all kinds of communities. Alua feels that rectifying the issue of inclusivity really rests within the mainstream Caucasian services that have identified they have a lack of diversity – where a problem is identified, the onus is on that service to fix it, to be actively seeking out diversity and making services more equitable and/or socially just. Alua holds the space and sets that example for many people coming into the end-of-life space, and she finds that by her presence in the space others in diverse communities show up and find ways they can be there too.

The American National Hospice and Palliative Care Organisation (NHPCO), created an End of Life Doula Council and are working to build bridges between doulas and many other EOL services, including medical ones. This Council started because Henry Fersko-Weiss and Deanne Cochrane (both well known

Alua Arthur, Olivia Bareham and myself at the doula gathering in Los Angeles, California, USA

people in the end-of-life space) were invited to do a talk at the NHPCO's annual conference and the feedback was such that there was huge interest in the role of doula and potentially, what they have to offer. NHPCO saw value in exploring this further, so the Council grew from there. They asked for applications from interested parties, Alua applied and was accepted and served a term on the Council. Importantly, the Council has not just doulas on it, it has hospice and palliative care staff members and representatives as well as social workers and other people with vested interest in this space.

The main role of the Council at present is to educate the members of the NHPCO and also the community about the role of the doula. In 2019 the Council offered a webinar designed for families to discuss their options and 1200 people signed up. The majority of those who signed up were workers and volunteers in the NHPCO space, which has highlighted that more education is needed for the carers first, before the families are reached in a meaningful way.

The hope and intention is that the Council will create the space for the role of the doula in end-of-life care, with paid positions in these places but also as a referral and contract style service to enable hospice and palliative staff to call on and refer outpatients to doulas who work privately.

Alua offers training that readies people to consider their own mortality. Having a legal background, she is well aware of the problem that can come when people are unprepared for death. She hopes that by engaging people in honest conversation they are able to more authentically consider their wishes.

Alua believes that micro-credentialing is a good and necessary step for the role of doula. It provides a level of legitimacy to what a doula has to offer and gives a form of standardisation to the work; a family can hire any doula and regardless of the ethos behind the training they have received, the family can be assured that the outcome and the quality of care the doula provides should be of the one high standard. No trainer is going to want to provide a course where the end result is that the doula is not equipped to pass the micro-credentialing accreditation. This puts everyone on a level playing field.

The hope is that micro-credentialing will build public confidence in the role of the doula and it means that doulas can have one message, which will also greatly assist with community education. It is always difficult to market a service with competing ideas and messages.

As a firm advocate for personal agency at the end of life, Alua works to build capacity within people to take control and give meaningful thought to end-of-life decisions and options. She is keenly aware of the difference this makes to people at the end of life and the enhanced grief and bereavement outcomes people have as a result.

Above and right: Views of the Hollywood Forever Cemetery, Los Angeles, USA

SACRED CROSSING

OLIVIA BAREHAM – CALIFORNIA, USA

http://sacredcrossings.com/artofdeathmidwifery/

Olivia, originally from the UK, is the owner of an alternative funeral home – Sacred Crossings Funeral Home, and has been living in Los Angeles and working in the end-of-life space for fifteen years. Many of the doulas in Los Angeles got their start with her as she provides doula training across America.

Having trained over 700 people, Olivia has now settled on a three-part model of education for her training and she finds her students are either people who are curious and/or who are afraid of death, or they are in the end-of-life movement and they want to learn more. She has found that people want to heal themselves of their own fear and trauma and that is why people come to her – it is part of a broader spiritual journey.

Sacred Crossing Funeral Home handles approximately 40 funerals per year. Many of the alternative/independent funeral homes in Los Angeles contract the services of a mortuary who do the transport, however Sacred Crossings Funeral Home do this themselves. They share a crematorium who provide refrigeration for the bodies and perform their cremations but as directors they do all of their own chemical-free body care.

Olivia's clients are able to keep the body of their person at home for up to three days. She often works with various multicultural communities for home funerals and has also been offering sea burials as a regular option for people for quite some time, which has proven popular. She works with a sea Captain who, when the time comes, shrouds and weights the body. They have to go six miles offshore before they can perform the burial. Olivia follows the Captain's boat with up to 150 people on a second witness boat where the ceremony is also held. The cost for this is US$2,900.00 (AUS$4,000.00) plus the shroud and her time. After the ceremony, the family get a certificate with the exact co-ordinates of the burial site so they can revisit for anniversaries and the like.

Olivia believes there should be doulas and midwifes in every hospital, that the value they bring to the end-of-life space enhances the experiences of the dying and their families. She is keen for the focus not to be lost –the family involvement and capacity is central to their experience of a good grief outcome.

INTERNATIONAL END OF LIFE DOULA ASSOCIATION (INELDA)

JERI GLATER AND JANIE RAKOW – NEW YORK, USA

https://www.inelda.org/

When Jeri Glater and Janie Rakow were doing this work in hospice (long before they started training anyone), they and their co-founder Henry Fersko-Weiss found they were being asked more and more to teach people how they approached and carried out their work. It was this feedback and community demand that gave them the impetus to start the training organisation which is the not-for-profit known as INELDA.

When they started their work with INELDA they saw it as a community and volunteer-based training, designed to increase community capacity. There has been so much growth and change in the last few years and they are now seeing that people who do the training want to be paid for the work (and ultimately want to establish themselves as a business) and overall they feel the community is responding well to that. INELDA have expanded their training to include further comprehensive training with this is mind.

Since its inception INELDA have also developed a good network between the doulas who train with them. They encourage those bonds and offer special content exclusively to those who have trained with them from time to time.

Aware of the shift to micro-credentialing, they have developed their own process by which proficiency is attained. INELDA has created a high bar for achieving this. To gain proficiency, doulas have to do 36 hours of work as a doula and reflect on their learning and experience. INELDA are looking for the hours to be served at three different phases of the end-of-life care. A doula is required to keep track of five different deaths they have attended, do two kinds of evaluations and keep timesheets of hours spent with clients. They also need to have a supervisory evaluation as well as a family evaluation from the people they have worked with.

The most heavily weighted requirement in their process is the ALR journal – active, listening, responding. Through this, INELDA get to see how the doula is managing, functioning and assisting the dying person and/or the family member. Additionally, the doula is called to do self-introspection through this time and journal that as well. There are requirements for a verbal exchange to be documented for approximately seven exchanges between the doula and the client which is then deconstructed and reflected upon. This helps to recognise what the role of doula really is and where skills can be developed and built upon.

INELDA makes a point of providing feedback on all of these assessment components to the doula. They consider this to be continuing education for the doulas as they enhance and grow their skill sets. Doulas are also required to keep a personal journal writing, about what they witness, experience and how they feel through this process. Included in the process of gaining credentials is a 'scope of practice' and a 'code of ethics' which the doula has to agree to and sign.

Achieving proficiency with INELDA is a lengthy process. The completion of this proficiency process can take from six months to three years before a doula reaches a position of successfully having achieved the INELDA micro-credentialing. At the conclusion of all of this, the doula is required to pass a final essay exam. Once achieved, the certification lasts for three years and re-certification can be done upon application.

The first training given by INELDA was in February 2015. Since then over 2000 people have undertaken their public training, although it is unclear how many are making a full-time income from this work. They also create programs and work with hospices and volunteer based organisations for doulas. They spend a lot of time providing community education in support of the market for their doulas. At the time of writing, INELDA had about 800 people who were in the process of gaining proficiency with them.

In the last few years of their work the narrative around death and the conversations we as a society are having has changed and things like death cafés are creating a positive impact. Palliative care as they know it in the USA is a space that is only 25 years old, but this care too has now changed their conversation. The population is ageing and living longer; people are looking for a better way to die. The people who would have used birth doulas are now at a different stage of life and in need of an end-of-life doula.

Jeri and Janie do foresee problems with a coming together of the wider doula movement; there are so many different rules state to state and country to country, so many different types of training and focuses. They would however like to see collaboration around skill and wisdom sharing; they acknowledge that there are so many people doing this around the world differently and doing it well, and we need to be able to share the capacity.

INELDA have also tried to address the issue of inclusivity, and to this end they offer pro bono training to those marginalised communities that need them, they offer training to people who cannot afford it as well as programs within diverse and/or disadvantaged communities. This has been the case for over three years now, looking at the various spaces where communities need them and working with charities and churches to provide their training – this has the effect of skilling people within a community to be able to look after their own.

INELDA has a doula directory with over 300 people on it. This is a public directory where people may find an INELDA trained doula located nearby.

INELDA promotes a group and team-based approach to end-of-life care. This is not always achievable and there are many solo doulas working alone in their communities, however more and more they find through the INELDA network that they are forming collectives.

Both Jeri and Janie were part of a team of doulas who have supported families, one of which was written about in the book *Caring for the Dying* by their co-founder, Henry Fersko-Weiss. In that case, they were part of a team of 13 doulas looking after one family, each of the doulas had their own gifts and skills they brought to the situation. One loved the night shift, another brought the gift of song.

Collectively they provided holistic care to the dying person and their family. Everyone supported each other and the family. They find that doulas are creating their own networks now to be able to form collaborative networks to learn and serve families together.

The training INELDA provides stops at the point of death. They do not teach about creating funerals or home body care. They agree that this is not the role of a doula. Ideally, a doula will come into the picture as early as possible and work with the dying all the way through the process so that upon death, the family have been aware of all of their choices already and most of the decisions will have already been made. None of this will include the doula providing after-death care to the body of the deceased.

Importantly, a doula from INELDA does not walk away at the point of death, and while they do not get involved in the planning of a funeral or the intimate body care, they are generally present and remain a support to the family through that process.

While they have developed and grown the focus that they originally set out with – which was to build the capacity within communities to look after the dead – that core tenet of their training remains unchanged.

FITTING TRIBUTE
AMY CUNNINGHAM – NEW YORK, USA
http://www.fittingtributefunerals.com/

Amy did not grow up wanting to be a funeral director. She came to the work through personal experience – it was the death of her dad that opened her eyes to the process of ceremony and how it could be so much better. Amy very much came from the perspective of a celebrant, with a background in writing. She wanted to be able to create beautiful and beneficial ceremonies for people where they would leave with a sense of peace.

Amy joined the funeral industry, making the decision to work within it to offer new, different and fitting tributes for people. She wanted to work with families who wanted to be a part of creating ceremony and ritual for their dead. Her small team has a more flexible approach and a strong environmental focus.

Fitting Tribute does not run its own mortuary; instead, she works with a Jewish funeral home who provides refrigeration if needed and performs any mortuary work if required. Amy used to do all the mortuary work herself but now only does as much as she has time for. She works with a transfer team to manage the transport of the deceased which allows her to be free to focus on the planning and delivery of the funeral ceremony.

Amy offers and encourages home funerals. She helps the family to bathe, dress and shroud the deceased in the family home or at the mortuary. She knows the value of people giving care to their dead. If the family choose not to be involved in the washing and dressing of their person, it will be done by the mortuary staff, however Amy asks that the staff do not seal the casket until she has 'met' the person.

Fitting Tribute is independent and consumer friendly, offering green and natural alternatives to families in products, services and options. Amy walks a sensible middle ground between the contemporary industry and the changing landscape that it finds itself in. She is open to all possibilities and by maintaining a family focus she finds she is best positioned to serve the needs of those she

From top: Amy Cunningham – Image courtesy Amy Cunningham;
Green-Wood Cemetery, Brooklyn; an indoor niche wall at Green-Wood Cemetery,
Brooklyn, New York, USA

works with, providing better grief and bereavement outcomes for them.

Fitting Tribute is not about doing the cheapest funerals, it is about unique experiences which both involve families and do not have to cost the earth. Amy works closely with Green-Wood Cemetery in New York, who are progressive in their approach to community, trying to do a lot of different activities and public events to stay current. They have a crematorium with various options for ashes interments as well as burial sites.

As a woman in her 60s, Amy sees herself as a bridge between the contemporary space and the more traditional approaches. Her main concern and focus is always the family and being in service to them; she is often working to invite the more traditional industry to consider the benefits of doing things differently. Through her writing and public engagements, she speaks about the changing landscape of funerals.

Amy's business is an example of an alternate approach working in the contemporary setting and she finds the families she serves have very healing experiences through the Fitting Tribute approach. Amy is also a prolific writer and has been gaining much publicity for her writing and her funeral work in recent years. As an advocate for families she works to normalise the experience because she believes in the benefits that can be gained by family-led approaches to death.

PART 4
COMMUNITY CAPACITY

Community capacity can be defined as a community, family and/or friendship group's ability to perform a task or approach any given issue with a level of knowledge, lived experience and confidence aimed at a successful outcome. In this section I will look at communities, organisations and projects whose object and purpose is to help people achieve this.

FROME, UK

https://www.discoverfrome.co.uk/frome/
https://www.compassionate-communitiesuk.co.uk/projects

Frome is a town that lives and breathes a level of community capacity that has been built over many years and is still growing, yet it is so normal that no one thinks anything of it.

Twenty years ago, Frome was an industrial mill town, where wool was its industry. By all accounts it was a hard, rough, low socio-economic and somewhat depressed place. It has been described to me as a fighting town: that was the reputation. Since then, this town has reinvented itself. There's an energy here that is unmatched in many places.

Every month there is an entire street in their town market dedicated to people starting new businesses, and the self-employed. People can register and turn up with a table to promote their ideas and sell their wares.

COMPASSIONATE COMMUNITIES

Compassionate Communities is a social care system that started in the town of Frome and the results have been phenomenal. This is a town where the residents take ownership over the responsibility of looking after each other.

Compassionate Frome had its roots deep within the community long before it had that name and well before it adopted the now global Compassionate Communities movement: the Frome Model of Care was created as a direct response to community need. This model was not initially developed on the Compassionate Community model but it was well placed to adopt it.

The original architects of the Frome Model of Care were Dr Helen Kingston and Jenny Hartnoll. What they created was the beginning of the movement which would become Compassionate Frome, once Dr Julian Abel (who was involved with Compassionate Communities) reached out and started working with them.

The monthly independent market, Frome, England

One of the first things they did was network mapping, expanding on the initial mapping that had already been done. Julie, an Area Lead within the Compassionate Frome Framework, had worked with Prof. Debbie Horsfall from Western Sydney University, Australia, to develop a way to undertake this mapping for the Frome Community.

The Compassionate Frome Framework works like this – there are dozens of community-minded people, called community connectors, who receive a very light training session which gives them basic knowledge and information on how to increase their awareness of what services exist in their community and how they can direct (called 'signposting') others to those services. They are able to signpost anyone to local services, friends, family, colleagues and neighbours – this becomes an active layer of support within their communities.

Community connectors are very effective at integrating with their local communities, providing a bridge between local people and other services, and building community knowledge. They know where they can signpost individuals to, for the support they need. Importantly, community connectors are not expected to have specialist knowledge or undertake any follow up.

The voluntary training of community connectors provided by people known as health connectors focuses on how to identify potential problems, concerns, struggles and issues within their fellow community members. The training includes what to look for, what questions to ask and how to approach conversations with people in their community. This on its own is a fantastic combative action against loneliness and other afflictions in the modern world, however it goes further. If the community connector finds there is someone they feel may be having a problem of some kind, they are able to make a referral back to a health connector located in the local medical centre.

Health connectors are paid positions and they take referrals from GPs and community connectors. They also work closely with local hospice services, hospital discharge teams and other end-of-life and age support services such as the Marie Curie nurses (who provide night nursing and support for home death), and Macmillan nurses (who help patients with cancer).

Once a referral is received, a health connector reaches out and makes a time to meet with the person referred to them. They use a social prescribing model to then refer that person on to various community services. Together they create plans and establish what the person's needs are. One of the plans they do is called a 'My Life Plan', which goes into detail looking at medications for a person, ensuring they understand what they are taking and why they are taking it. The plan also asks a person what they want to happen if they get ill and they briefly touch on death, but this is only really in relation to whether or not they have made arrangements for after death and where they want to be when they die.

Health connectors are able to signpost people to other services and charities. Interestingly, doulas are not on that referral list, even when someone is dying. The UK is similar to Australia in that various places provide doula-style training and some health connectors have doulas as personal friends. That professional connection, however, has not yet been made.

When I asked about how this community capacity translated to the end of life there was not a firm answer. It seems that Compassionate Frome, while being revolutionary for living a good life to the end and encompassing incredible capacity building within a community, does not do death or after-death any differently than the rest of the UK. The consensus among those I spoke to was that not everyone knows the options when it comes to dying and even more so after death. This is a gap that some people have more recently identified and in October 2019 Frome hosted its first festival about death called 'Pushing up Daisies' with a view to start the conversation on a more public scale.

The ripples for this radical approach to ageing well and living well continue to spread. At the time of writing there are six health connectors in Frome (paid positions) and they are also now in Glastonbury, Wells and Street. Frome Medical Centre is where it began and it is the centre of Compassionate Frome.

The following is a basic chart of the Compassionate Frome structure.

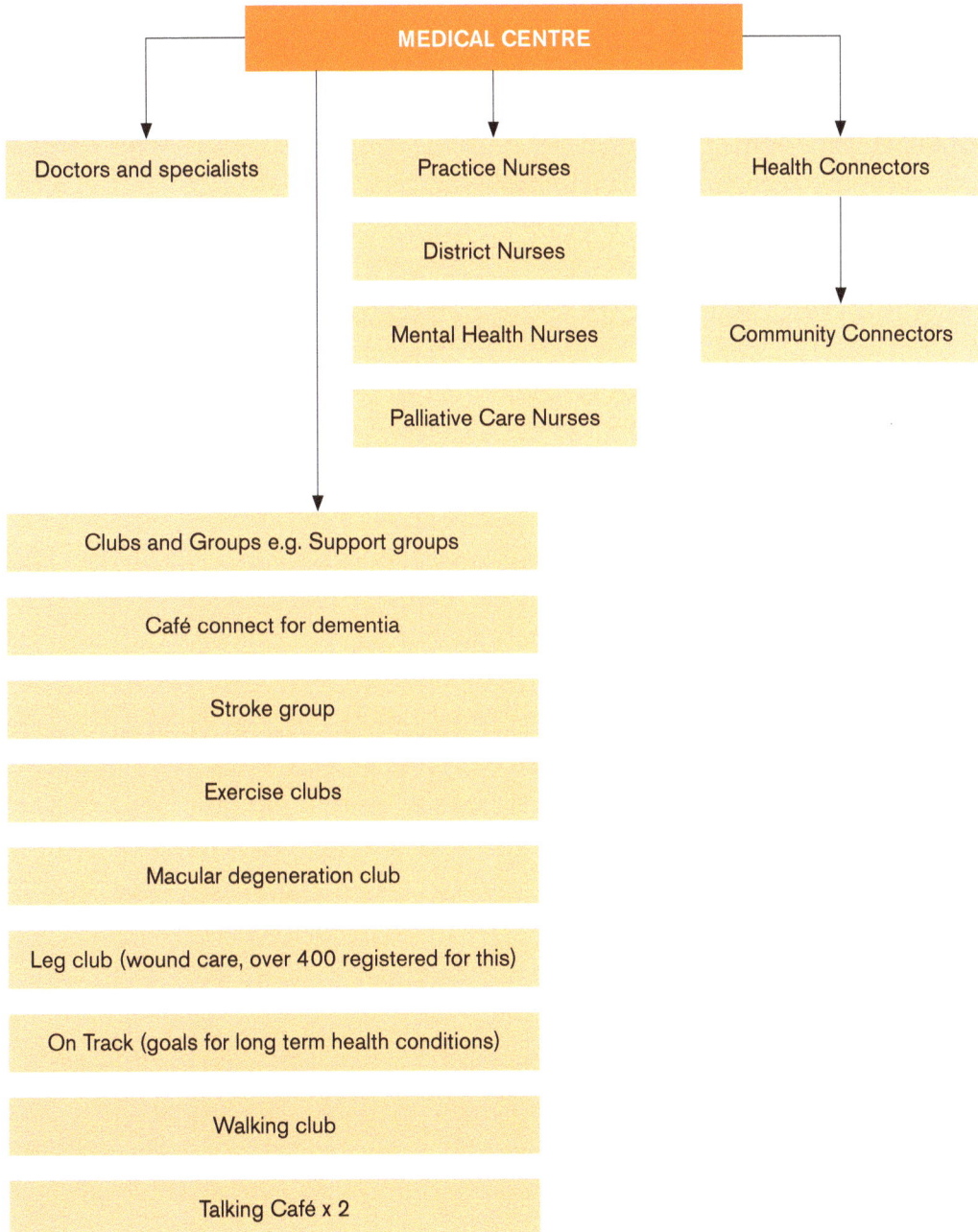

MEDICAL CENTRE

Doctors and specialists

Practice Nurses

Health Connectors

District Nurses

Community Connectors

Mental Health Nurses

Palliative Care Nurses

Clubs and Groups e.g. Support groups

Café connect for dementia

Stroke group

Exercise clubs

Macular degeneration club

Leg club (wound care, over 400 registered for this)

On Track (goals for long term health conditions)

Walking club

Talking Café x 2

Julie has trained over 1130 community connectors across the various communities. All Frome Police officers, local kids in the community and all the staff at their local Job Centre get her training, in the last case so that they are able to identify needs within their clients. She has also trained people in the Gypsy travelling communities and the Glastonbury 'off the grid' communities, groups that are often not necessarily able to access information about what services are available to them. In this way connectors are reaching a much wider population.

The origins of Compassionate Frome, prior to the connection with Compassionate Communities was one of a conscious move towards capacity building, right from the start. It was in 2013 that Dr Helen Kingston realised that people were coming to see her as a GP but did not necessarily need to see the doctor. Helen had Jenny map out what services were existing in the community and where the gaps were. To start with, the list was too long, so they decided to concentrate on those services local to Frome and with a presence in the town. The first thing they did was establish a Talking Café to start promoting conversation and connections within their community and this is still going strong.

Soon after they began, a man living with Multiple Sclerosis (MS) approached them, highlighting that there were no services available for people with MS. Jenny and Helen responded by gathering all the people they could with MS to ask them what was needed. Overwhelmingly, an exercise group was requested, which continues today and now has expanded to include people with different levels of ability and all kinds of illnesses. This socially driven approach to care has continued and remains an integral part of their compassionate community. If a person in the community feels a need for a group to be started, they can go to the health connectors who will work with appropriate stakeholders to set it up. Some work, some do not, but the important thing is that people are listened to.

'Social Prescribing' is a referral system that is not medically based. The health connectors in Frome were doing this long before it had a name. There is some concern that as it becomes an accepted and adopted process in government and private practice institutions, it will lose the value and effectiveness that it currently has at a grassroots level. One of the ways this could happen would be through the provision of financial incentives for social prescriptions. Frome is very clear that this is not an option. There are benefits, however to government involvement in the process. Until recently the funding for Compassionate Frome's health connectors has been on a six to twelve-month basis – they have continually lived with financial uncertainty. Partly because of this social prescribing system, they have since secured funding for 10 years.

Doctors are starting to hold group consultations – getting together patients all with the same conditions and addressing them from medical and social perspectives. The Frome Medical Centre also hosts weekly multidisciplinary meetings which involve home care workers, home first representatives, social workers, GPs, a citizen advice representative (a community member) as well as the local hospice and various charities. In this way everyone stays informed of the direction, initiatives and progress of each service. It provides the opportunity for accountability, clarity and peer support. Additionally, they hold a weekly palliative care meeting which one of the health connectors generally attends, which focuses on building the families' capacity to care for their dying.

Waiting lists have been getting shorter in Frome for Outer Social Care package services (similar to our aged care packages in Australia), but in the rest of the UK they are getting longer. This reduction has been attributed to the work the health connectors are doing, identifying needs and eligibility and connecting people to necessary services outside the government system.

The results of the cost-benefit analysis done on the Frome Model have had the world come knocking on the door of Frome Medical Centre. There have been huge financial savings from decreased presentations to the emergency department at Frome Hospital due to this uniquely preventative, social-based approach to care.

All these unique approaches are not without their criticisms. Some people in the community who did not want to be explicitly identified, were open to telling me that while the preventative model is fantastic in the most part, the increased traffic at the medical centre has made it nearly impossible to see a doctor at short notice if a person is sick, short of calling an ambulance.

People can no longer walk in and present at the medical centre to see a doctor, rather you have to call first and tell them what is wrong and that goes through an over-the-phone triage process where a doctor may call you before you get an appointment. They were quick to point out though, that if you were triaged as serious, you did very quickly receive the medical attention you needed.

Health Connections Mendip where many medical services and Compassionate Frome are based, Frome, England

TALKING CAFÉ

I attended a Talking Café which I had initially thought to be a Death Café. When I asked, the answer was pretty clear: the focus here is not death. Instead it is more of a social meeting for all kinds of people and topics. And it was indeed broad in terms of the range of people attending, levels of ability, age groups and very even mix in terms of men and women. There were people who attended who were living with illness, people recently bereaved and those caring for the ill – death was everywhere but no one was talking about it.

It soon became clear as I listened and engaged with the people attending, that while death was present in the minds of many of these people, the conversation was a focus on the living.

I met with Rose, who is a health connecter in Frome and the convenor of the Talking Café. She painted me a picture of how it all worked. Rose and Hannah were the two health connectors present to facilitate the group, but they do not facilitate the discussions. Beyond engaging with people who perhaps were not talking to others, their role is a beautifully supportive but largely passive one. They attend primarily to signpost people to services if they identify a need.

ACTIVE AND IN TOUCH

Active and In Touch is a charity in the UK, based in Frome and funded jointly through the local Frome Town Council, a lot of hard-working people who engage in fundraising and the incredible generosity of many of their volunteers.

Active and In Touch was started in 2011 by Anna Brindal, who saw a need in the community to combat isolation and loneliness. This was two years earlier than the start of Compassionate Communities project in Frome. I was introduced to a representative, Diane, who walked me through the service offerings.

Active and In Touch are very innovative and dynamic in their approach to the two services they offer to anyone aged 18 and over. Their main service is be-friending – a one-on-one service to address social isolation.

Through a model of social prescription, they receive referrals from lots of people: concerned community members, health connectors and GPs alike. Once they receive the referral either Diane or her colleague will meet with the person referred to them (known as the member) to get a sense of what interests them and what sort of volunteer they could be paired with. Active and In Touch have a bank of volunteers they can call on, although due to recent changes to their NHS they have an increased number of referrals who need to wait some time for a volunteer to become available.

When a match is made, there are no hard and fast rules for the be-friending. The contact between the volunteer and the member is usually weekly but it is always governed by people themselves and what they feel comfortable with.

The volunteers all receive training and Active and In Touch also offer special dementia training for those volunteering with members affected by the disease. In their training they are told not to hand out their personal details, however they have found some long term volunteer/member relationships have grown into complete and beautiful friendships. Diane knows that if the charity shut down tomorrow many of them would continue being close friends. The activities and outings, the scope of the be-friending between volunteers and members are very much up to them.

Active and in Touch also run social groups through the week. Some are art/craft based and others more social. The volunteer and member can attend one of those or they may want to go shopping, get the groceries, see a movie

Hunting Raven bookshop, Frome, England

or sit and chat over a cup of tea. In all of Diane's seven years in her role, only twice has she had a pairing not work out.

Active and In Touch has a series of raised garden beds at community garden plots where their members can go and get involved and through that they are now offering a paddock-to-plate style of community workshop where people grow the vegetables and learn how to cook with them. It culminates in a community feast!

If Active and In Touch receive a referral (or signpost) and they feel the person is not a fit for their offering, they are able to further signpost people if they cannot help them. They do this in addition to their service if they think the member would benefit from another service as well as their own. There seemed to be not a hint of competition between services, the focus being always on the outcomes for the member.

I asked if they ever got together in bigger groups – yes, that happens too. The service providers all have regular meetings, so they always know what the others are up to and this helps with the interconnection between them as well as the continuity of support for clients.

New groups have sprung from Active and in Touch. They have begun together and through gathering and identifying a common ground they have since split off independently. One such group was 'WOW' which supports widows and widowers. This is social capital and capacity in the making, whereby people gain the confidence through their program to start services and community groups of their own.

FLAT PACK DEMOCRACY

Frome is a town where people not only look after each other but they have taken control of the local government as well. Peter Macfadyen has written a book called 'Flat Pack Democracy', in which he describes how a group of interested locals kicked out partisan politicians in favour of a system that takes care of residents first.

In the UK, the levels of government are: National Government, County Government, District Government and then the local Parishes and Towns governance. In Frome that looks like: UK Government, Somerset County, Mendip District and the Frome Town Council.

A few years ago they decided to take back their town from party politics by gathering a group of independent people who were concerned only with the town of Frome, and together they made an independent party that has been continually elected in one way or another since it began. In May 2017 the party won all 17 seats on the Town Council and have maintained that ever since. They are following the model of Flat Pack Democracy which Peter designed.

Here is a town where the community all vote on what they want the Town Council funds to be used for. There is a high voting rate here in Frome; people appreciate the engagement. This system sees a huge percentage of revenue ploughed back into the community and into local projects to benefit residents. Many of the successful local projects and initiatives have had their start with the backing of this Council, adding to the capacity building in the town.

OTHER THINGS IN FROME

This is a town where everyone seems to want to help each other.

So I was told about a local bookseller, Tina, who had started a 'reading against loneliness' program. The way it works is simple. An appointment is booked

The community fridge and wardrobe where people can donate to and take from as needed, Frome, England

with her at the bookshop and when they arrive Tina spends time and reads with the person. They talk about all kinds of things over a cup of tea, including their reading and their life. Tina likes to find out about a person's life and interests and recommends reading material for them.

I spoke to Tina to find out a little more. It turns out that Pan Macmillan had given six grants to bookstores in the UK and hers was lucky enough to receive one, for her community initiatives. She has two parts to her grant. One is the one-on-one reading, where she sits and talks to people over tea and cake and gets to know about their life etc. and Tina gives them a book to take home as well.

The other part to the grant was a one-off party she hosted at the end of September 2019 which was designed to engage and bring together people who are suffering more hidden loneliness – young people, single parents, those who perhaps do not fit the standard models of what loneliness looks like. This is important as loneliness is being considered a large contributor to early deaths in the western world. Tina brought all kinds of people together in a party setting to create connections and encourage conversations. Everyone was asked to bring along a book that meant something to them as a conversation starter. And what would a Compassionate Community be without a community fridge!

It is believed that this was the first community fridge in the UK. Since its inception, it has become so popular that the local supermarkets now send food there regularly and I am told the fridge is always full. I was surprised to see that it was also a community clothing rack where the community can come and take whatever they need.

When I visited the fridge (and the community clothing rack beside it) a lady there told me she had recently moved to Frome and was trying to get herself established. We chatted and she told me of the generosity and good will she has encountered since moving here. She was so impressed with everyone welcoming her so warmly and with all of the services she had been directed to which had not been available elsewhere.

I also spoke to a man by the name of Jim. He is a volunteer who collects food each day from local businesses and delivers it to the food bank. He told me that seven of them volunteer to collect the goods from different shops in Frome. As we were talking, a man approached to donate an entire crate of bread that was left over from the market held that day in town.

During my wanderings in the market, I met Bryce from a Christian organisation called HOPE. HOPE is an initiative of FACT – Frome Area Christians Together. Even the different churches have come together in Frome to work for the benefit of the town and its people. They run many combined welfare initiatives including a caravan for coffee. This portable quiet space for people to gather can be driven to late-night venues and hot spots in town.

And then there's Lisa's Army. Lisa's Army started when a young mum, Lisa, who had been diagnosed with bowel cancer, decided to raise money and support for her family to help them after she died. When I visited the tribute to her in the centre of town, the flowers were not yet dead – an incredible outpouring of love and support in tribute to this young life so recently lost to cancer. At the time of writing Lisa's Army were still raising funds for her family and the community love and support was overwhelming. The flowers are representative of the real and tangible help her family had been receiving.

As an example of the community-centred mentality of Frome, it is well worth noting that when I met the host of my Airbnb accommodation, Elaine, she said that she was not really involved in the Compassionate Communities. She proceeded over the next few days to take me around town, introducing me to the various people she knew to be involved in it. I discovered quite quickly that while she does not see herself as involved on Compassion Communities, she actually lives it. Elaine has been involved in the setup of Independent for Frome, having served terms as both a town Councillor and Mayor. She was involved as a volunteer helping to settle refugee families in Frome and she was aware of and in touch with a lot of people who were able to help me, 'signposting' me in the right direction.

Frome has reclaimed its government and its media. The local Frome paper concentrates on all the positive news. Everything here is by locals, for locals. The heart of community. They reclaimed their market for entrepreneurs. They have dozens of community initiatives and social justice projects, outreach programs and many varied and beautiful layers of people looking after people. They may not have succeeded in reclaiming death but they are the benchmark of what to strive for in life.

CRESTONE, COLORADO USA

Crestone is a town with incredible community capacity who have reclaimed much of their way of life from an otherwise less community-focused world. This is a community of people who look after each other. Even just sitting in a café, I heard both customers and employees talk about the CEOLP, educating newcomers to the town about what is available.

This is a community network in action. As a beautiful symbol of the freedom felt in this town, the deer roam free here. They are on the side of the road, in the main street – they seem to live everywhere. You can see them and chipmunks at every turn.

Crestone is a place that allows for the ego to be stripped away and people to be comfortable being who they are without fear of judgement. It is a true melting pot of people, cultures, backgrounds, faiths and beliefs and they all coexist in harmony. There is no police presence here; the community works on a basis of respect and helping each other.

There is incredible social focus – there is a café called 'Our Food is our Art', there's local media, dozens of volunteer groups and co-ops, about 60 art studios, shops selling local crafts and hand made goods, a 'free box' (which is a space people can donate things for others to pick up to use), a food bank system, and in nearly every shop, community notice boards offer people ways of communicating and coming together.

In Crestone you can find several book clubs, art groups and classes and at least two or three community gardens. They have a system of carers for the sick and elderly and while the town does have an ambulance, the nearest hospital or pharmacy is an hour away so having a system of care is very important.

There is a local threshold choir who sing to the sick and dying, providing a very tangible kind of peace, comfort and healing energy. I was able to sit in on one

A deer wandering the street of the town in Crestone, Colorado, USA

of their 'sound baths' and it was a serene and peaceful experience. Crestone has an extensive list of resources and services available to this relatively small community of people.

Crestone is high desert country, cold at night and hot through the day. There are adobe and straw bale homes, most are solar passive, and many of the residents in and around Crestone are living off the grid. According to James McCaplin[5], Crestone is built on philanthropy. Commercialisation could not succeed there, but community did.

In 1977 Maurice Strong and his partner Hanne acquired a company called AZL Resources and the unsold land around Crestone came with it. The intent for this land was designed around commercial ventures and the subdivision had been earmarked for a retirement village. It soon became apparent that this would not work.

In 1978 a long-time local mystic named Glenn Anderson knocked on Hanne's door and told her he had been waiting for her. He told her of a prophecy from the Indigenous Americans, about this land being a place of healing and that she would unite the various wisdom keepers of the world here. In 1979 and 1980 Hanne met with various elders to confirm the prophecy and eventually she and Maurice were convinced so they went about splitting up the land and donating it to various faith and belief groups. There are now over 30 of these spread between the mountains, foothills and the plains around Crestone. There are Japanese, Buddhist (Tibetan, Zen etc.), Yoga Ashrams and many other faith communities represented in this place. People make a pilgrimage here from all over the world. Some of them have stayed and thus a community was born.

The CEOLP is an umbrella organisation under which many varied but necessary facets of the end-of-life journey from death to disposal take place. To this end, CEOLP is split up into roles. Upon death they have roles such as a facilitator, a care of body team, a fire team, a post-burn team. All these different groups of volunteers mobilise upon learning of the death of someone who is registered with CEOLP. Each group has a team leader and all the volunteers receive training and oversight.

One of the things important to CEOLP is the knowledge that families have the right to transport the body of their person over state lines. This is important because if someone who is registered with CEOLP dies while away, they can always be bought back for cremation.

CEOLP have built enduring relationships with the various stakeholders required to make their services possible – the sheriff's department, coroner, property owner's association and the fire department. A lot of time and energy has gone into setting up firm and consistent policy and procedures to ensure seamless service provision.

Informed Final Choices (IFC), an end-of-life education service, is another of the resources available for residents in Crestone. They have a community library and they have had around 20–30 people turning out to events such as death cafés.

IFC are able to charge for services such as workshops and seminars as well as receive donations, and gradually they are growing. IFC and CEOLP have separate boards but many of the same people are on them and they meet together. The board roles are volunteer based, not decided by a vote.

In Colorado, the coroner is responsible for signing off on every death. The coroner for this county has been very supportive and worked with the CEOLP to help them achieve their goals. Colorado has a 72-hour rule in terms of the

From top: The Crestone End of Life Project / Informed Final Choices Library;
Crestone Cemetery, Crestone, Colorado, USA

body being kept at home and after that time disposal needs to take place. They use regular ice packs to keep the bodies cool in the home. It took a long time to educate the community and governments to get all of the necessary permissions in place, and long-time resident Stephanie Gaines was integral to this stage of CEOLP's development.

CEOLP is based on transparency. Families are made aware of the after-death care process and can be as involved as they would like to be. When CEOLP get a call that someone has died a facilitator is immediately assigned to the family. Facilitators are trained in both the logistical aspects of death care and cremation, the legalities and the paperwork, processes etc., but they also provide an integral role in delegation and mobilisation. They mobilise the 'care of the body' teams, the fire teams etc. They liaise with the team leaders of each area of service – they do not take on any roles outside their scope. That is one of the reasons this works – everyone knows their roles. They receive training and mentoring, and they all work together.

The facilitator puts in place the logistics and deals with all of the departments and the neighbours. They are also the conduits for direct contact with the family and team leaders. They assign the Master of Ceremonies (who will work with the family to create the ceremony) as well as designate the coordinator for the ceremonial aspects. It is a good part of a whole day's work by the time the facilitator has put everything that is required in place. A desire to be of service is key to the successful outcome of this process. By being voluntary, they feel as though they retain the integrity of a community being of service to each other.

Crestone also has a 40-acre public cemetery, five acres of which have been put aside for green burial. CEOLP supports families who would like green burial although that is not their primary focus. Because the origins of CEOLP were focused on open-air cremation as the main disposition choice, they are still improving their volunteer knowledge and training to support green burials more fully and educating the community about how CEOLP can support community members who choose green burials.

Families and community members do have the option to dig the graves themselves in that cemetery however it is often left to the excavator to dig and fill in the graves. This is highly recommended, as the ground is very rocky and difficult to dig by hand and there is a requirement that the site is restored to a 'natural state'.

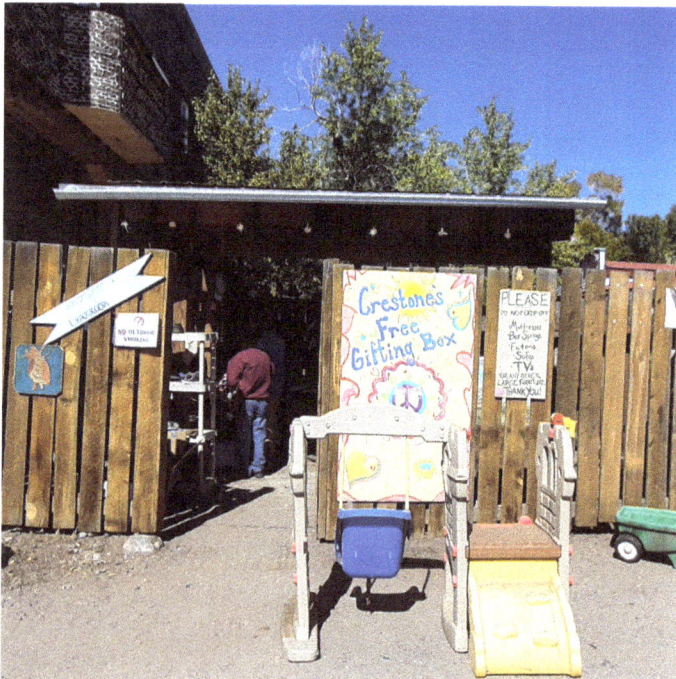

From top: The Altar built for display items at funeral ceremonies held at the Pyre site; Crestone's Free Gifting Box, a swap point for all kinds of goods in the township, Crestone, Colorado, USA

If CEOLP is called to provide support with home funeral and green burial assistance, they help the family determine what is desired within the scope of green burial guidelines. A person who was registered with CEOLP will have recorded their wishes before death and include things such as their choice of a shroud or a natural container, untreated wooden coffin as part of their registration process. In this way they are also doing their own version of death-care planning.

More recently CEOLP set aside another parcel of land near their pyre site which will be exclusively a natural burial ground, run with the same volunteer model they use for cremation. The natural burials to date have been done very simply, with wide wooden planks and straps for lowering. They have tried various techniques over the years, including excavating a sloped earth ramp into the grave, but there are some parts to the new offering under development. What will not be missing is the care and commitment the CEOLP have towards creating a beautiful and peaceful interment for their community members.

Allison Wonderland is a woman with remarkable capacity and talent. She has volunteered in many of the roles in the CEOLP, including the fire team and body care team and she is also involved in the natural burial section of the Crestone cemetery. Of working with the fire team Allison says –

> *My experiences with CEOLP fire team have been deeply moving. I have had many varied experiences. While each time is unique, there are some common experiences through all. There is the sense of the honour and privilege of serving, a fellowship between the fire team/whole CEOLP team and the community, a presence of mystery and grace, and the awe of the phenomenal natural and elemental presence. There is a creative aspect, problem-solving different things that come up, remaining in respect and being as simple and calm as possible.[6]*

The role of the fire team lead is integral to the successful cremation but also the successful outcome and experience for the family and community. CEOLP organise this team with a great deal of consideration, including the coordination of who will be on the fire team and the preparation of the site the day before, all while training volunteers who are learning. Allison says,

> *The fire team tries to remain respectful, subtle and discreet throughout, while keeping the fire at a high temperature, even burning, using logs*

etc. to refrain from any body exposure, and using juniper to reduce odours. I followed the basic CEOLP protocol for becoming a fire team volunteer. I began with a general familiarity with CEOLP as a whole through attending monthly meetings, reading thru the website, and witnessing the fire team during cremations. I attended the trainings specific for fire team volunteers, and then 'shadowed' – was a fire team-in-training during cremations. Over time, I became more accustomed to the work, developing skills and deepening relationships with the other fire team members. Paul, an original CEOLP founder and Fire Team Leader, began asking me to be the Fire Team Coordinator. I have worked all three shifts.[7]

Allison has had a wide variety of experiences with care of the body over the last 20 years, through family beloveds, working as a hospice aide in the state of Massachusetts, as a private duty caregiver and death midwife for many years, as well as through CEOLP.

The CEOLP training included first becoming generally familiar with CEOLP organization/going to meetings etc., then taking the trainings specific to care of the body, which are a few hours and include going thru the manual instructions as well as hands-on role playing and becoming familiar with the care of the body basket.[8]

The body care team support the family to be as hands-on and involved with the care of a person's body, as they are comfortable to be.

Crestone is a community that has reclaimed its capacity from many of the conventional social systems and in doing so they have embraced end-of-life and death care as well. Everyone acknowledges the benefit of doing this. People everywhere spoke of feeling supported and a part of something very special being in the service of others. There was a true sense of community spirit between these people and genuine concern for each other.

Top right: An alter of friendship and remembrance at the 2019 National Home Funeral Alliance Conference

DEATH TALK PROJECT
HOLLY PRUETT, USA
http://deathtalkproject.com/

Holly Pruett trained as a home funeral guide over a decade ago with Jerrigrace Lyons and at that time she became aware of the many different conversations around death and dying. She became involved as the death cafés got off the ground in the USA and started the first one in Portland Oregon.

She decided they should do a festival around the end-of-life space, and it took a year to put together a town square-style event where people could come, mingle and talk. The event was hugely successful with 10 hours of programming for US$40.00 per ticket. They had about 70 different presenters including a keynote from Stephen Jenkinson. All 500 tickets were sold and at the end of it all they had 170 people on the wait list.

Holly has a particularly refreshing view. She sees individuality as being tied up with class and through that, the commodification of the industry around death. In North America there has been so much happening around death – making it sexy and hip. People are considering how they can have the 'best death' as an expression of their individuality.

In a way, Holly explains, some people are approaching death as a self-improvement project. While that is not inherently bad, it is flawed because there is very little focus on what our death can do for the community. We are largely a secular society and collectively we do not have a lot of stories about how to approach this new way of looking at death.

Instead of seeing a death ritual as something to benefit a community and their grief, death is turned into something providing personal comfort, something individual. More recently there have also been commercial issues – Holly wonders, who can afford a designer death, or a re-do of what was quite often already an expensive ceremony.

Holly says we need better stories about death and how our deaths can serve the greater good. People come to the conversations about death with very little experience or having just had a very personal one. They are often encouraged to take some kind of action, such as becoming a volunteer with a hospice, but there are a lot of people in need who are left out of those systems of care, and we need to find ways to reach them too.

The Death Talk Project began when she was approached by a donor who wanted to fund her work, so she settled on a project designed to get communities talking to each other about death. Holly created a space where people could have an event such as a movie screening and facilitated conversation to follow. In addition to this she had been doing a twice-monthly newsletter, blogging and raising discussion questions. After about three years she moved away from the events and others have since taken that over.

Holly decided that there needed to be something for Oregon citizens that made the information about what is legally possible and how to do home funerals available for all the communities in her state. She created Oregon Funeral Resources and Education, a website focused on increasing people's ability to inform each other and their own communities about how to care for each other in this space.

When considering the work of this movement and her work within it, Holly's best outcome is a normalisation of death-caring capacity in families and communities. We do not need more specialists or experts in death care. Death care, ritual and practice is not something that needs to be professionalised, fetishised or made special. It should be considered another part of how families are looking after each other.

Late night writing and research in between interviews

Holly believes that people in this space need to come from a place where ceremony is more of an everyday maintenance and a contribution to building an overall healthier cultural story, rather than being treated as a special event for a single moment. By making ceremony special to singular occasions we have cut death out of the fabric of our everyday story.

If those working in the space of death literacy build people's capacity to look after the dead, they can choose to hire a professional because they want one, not because they need one. This is in stark contrast to where many people find themselves, the otherwise all too common position of hiring a professional as a coping strategy against grief.

In Holly's experience, the 'doing' of death care themselves always brings a better outcome for families and their communities.

NEW ORLEANS

In New Orleans I wandered the graveyards, explored the unique heritage and spoke to various community members including Valerie Armand, a doula, and Brooke, a funeral director.

VALERIE ARMAND – DOULA AND HOSPICE WORKER

Valerie has spent a long time in the end-of-life space and has more recently come to doula work. I was surprised to learn that home funerals are not very common in New Orleans. A great many of the ideas people have about New Orleans and their connection to death really exist in ceremony only, and not much of it is family led.

In New Orleans a body must either be embalmed, disposed of, or refrigerated within 72 hours of death. This is a rule I found to be not uncommon across the USA. This is one of the reasons attributed not only to the process of embalming but also to why bodies do not commonly stay in the home. The general process when someone dies is simply embalming, visitation, ceremony then disposal. All of this is governed by funeral directors. There is usually a longer time between the death and ceremony than is common in other places and families will often wait days until a weekend for the ceremony.

Perhaps the best known New Orleans tradition is that of the Jazz Funeral, the famous street parades to honour the dead. They are called '2nd lines' and they happen not only during funerals but during weddings and other major milestones within New Orleans communities. They happen anywhere around local neighbourhoods, not just through the famous Bourbon Street.

There are families who make visible statements with t-shirts or hats with the deceased's face on them. Everyone wears these, and these bold and public gestures are perhaps where some people find agency in the funeral process. All of this is about their community's connection to each other, and there is a bonding over ceremony in many different ways. At the same time, however, there is a real distance from the body of the deceased and the reality of their death.

Valerie says that people largely have their heads in the sand in regard to the realities of the end of life in New Orleans: there is not a lot of pre-planning. People do the big ceremonial services but will not talk about death before it happens and they do not have much interaction with the body at all. Recently this has been challenged in a few select and very public ways where the 'posing' of some deceased has taken place. This is where a body is embalmed and posed to look alive, often in an upright position, and doing something they enjoyed in life. It has been met with mixed results.

In Valerie's experience the African-American community has a very raw expression of grief and sometimes anger at the deathbed. They are not afraid to display a vulnerable and very public outpouring of emotion – as a community they collectively share the burden of it. But still, no one talks about death before it happens.

Among other cultural groups she has worked with, Valerie finds the Asian and Hispanic communities (who are very under-represented in the hospice world), are also afraid of death and even change doctors when they have suggested it is time for a move to hospice care.

Another factor Valerie pointed out, that is not to be discounted across America, is that there are a lot of 'illegal' people who are without papers, and so do not put themselves forward to receive much needed services, choosing instead to risk going without. Death for these people is largely unseen by most others, and they do not have anyone to talk to about their end of life or any agency within the process – there are absolutely no cultural considerations made for them.

There is a huge brand loyalty with people who use the same funeral home they have been using for many generations. There is even a racial split that exists where people of colour will only use certain funeral homes just like some religious groups will favour one funeral home over the other.

In Valerie's hospice role she finds there are a lot of older men who are trying to live independently. They have safety issues, but they have no one else to turn to and will not leave their homes. Staff are left only two options: either to report the person as a potential safety concern, or to discharge them from services and send them home. There are issues around lines of responsibility when it comes to sending someone to go home and often people are not willing to take what is considered to be the risk in doing this.

Valerie says that in the wider community a similar fear can be found; at times people don't really like to check on their neighbours for fear of being responsible or blamed if something goes wrong. It is into this space that a doula could be very helpful; it is a space that could well benefit from a Compassionate Communities approach.

BROOKE, FUNERAL DIRECTOR IN NEW ORLEANS

Many ways of celebrating have been melded together in New Orleans, and it could be fair to say that some have been overshadowed by the growth of people celebrating the Mexican tradition of Dias de los Muertos. All Saints Day, however, which is celebrated on 1 November in New Orleans, has traditionally been the most popular local ceremony (not to be confused with All Souls Day). All Saints Day was always a big deal, but more recently it seems to be fading.

There was a time in New Orleans when 1 November was the day where people used to spend their time in the cemetery cleaning, painting and fixing the graves of their dead, but this is not as common now. Every year on that day, Brooke goes with a preservationist to give cookies to the cemetery workers and talk to people, to share time and knowledge with them. She would like to see a return to this fading tradition; it is a connection with the dead she is keen to be kept. Brooke wants to engage the younger people in these traditions of caring for the graves of our dead. Brooke is also pro-green funeral.

There is no fully dedicated space for natural burial in Louisiana and there are only a few places where a handful of sites have been made available for this style of burial. Even though it is possible to do a natural burial in Louisiana, those spaces are few and far between. The cremation rate is climbing in New Orleans and the market is still – somewhat surprisingly – traditional. The home funeral movement is not really accepted among older people, and the younger people are only recently starting to open up to the necessary conversations.

Brooke makes an effort to visit groups and death cafés to talk to people and see what is going on for them. She finds that often she ends up answering a whole lot of questions, not just legal but also emotional questions, as well as the ones that people have for whatever reason, felt they could not ask before. For a community that hosts a Museum of Death, traditions of voodoo, vampires

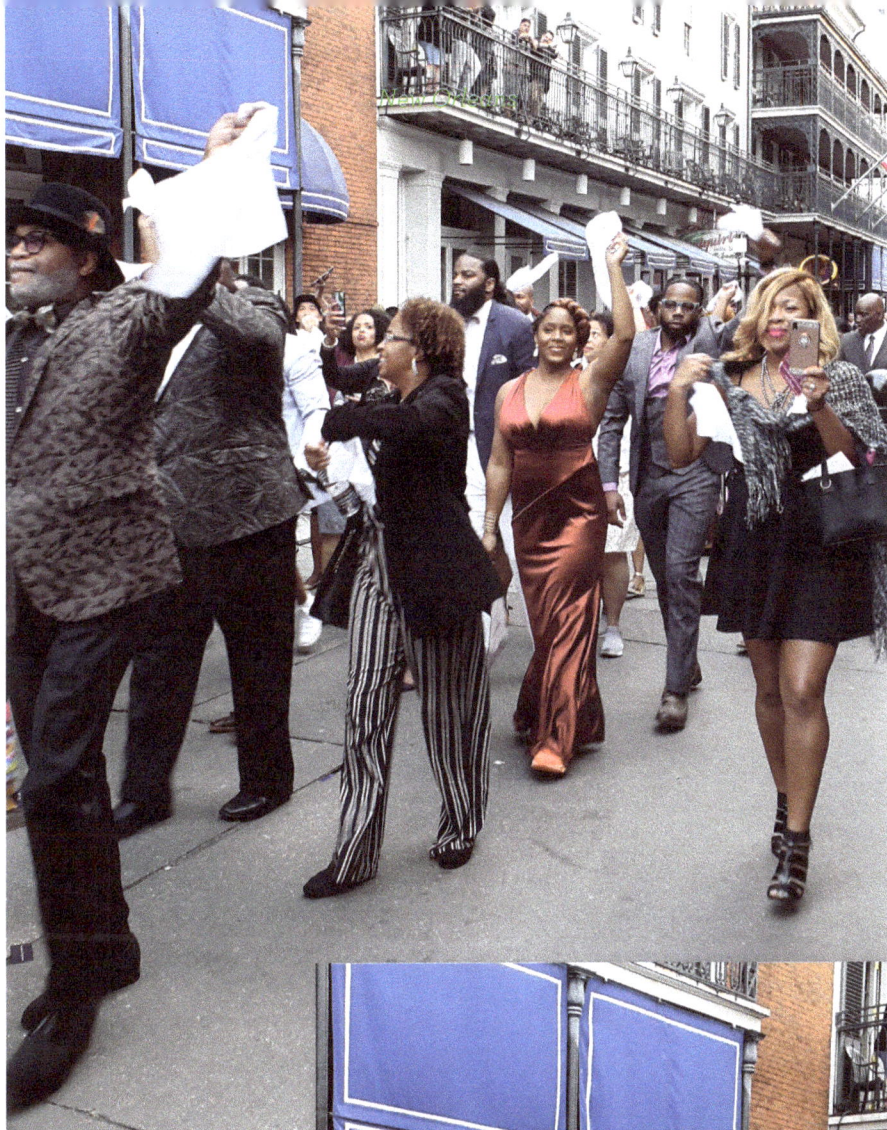

A jazz wedding procession
in the French Quarter,
Bourbon Street,
New Orleans, USA

Graves in St Joseph's Cemetery, New Orleans, USA

and other sensational death related curiosities, the lack of actual death literacy is astounding.

In Louisiana, the funeral industry has an 'E' licence and a 'U' licence, embalming and undertaking. Not every funeral director (with a 'U' licence) is an embalmer. In Louisiana a funeral director is legally required for both custody of the body and the filing of the death certificate. So, if a body is to stay at home the approval of the funeral home must be on record. Generally, if the body is going to be at home for any length of time, the funeral directors will first take and embalm the body and deliver it back to the home afterwards.

Brooke takes issue with people telling families that embalming is necessary for public viewing; it is often policy, but not law. She feels that embalming is so common that people fear what an un-embalmed body looks like, simply because they have never seen one, and she would like people to be more informed. Brooke thinks there needs to be more communication between the industry and the home funeral movement.

Having a very intimate knowledge of the burial practices in New Orleans, Brooke was able to share with me how they are done. There is a lot of assumption and misconception around how burials are done in places like New Orleans and while the world believes one thing, the reality is vastly different.

To start with, there are usually multiple burials in the one in-ground tomb site in their historical cemeteries. The tombs are designed to breathe and flex. There is a two-tomb structure on top of the ground but under it is a 6-feet pit (this depth varies). This is why there are dozens of names listed as buried in the one tomb. Historically, there were also society tombs, using the same concept.

The floor at the bottom of the tomb is slatted and remains are placed or pushed into the bottom chamber, clearing space ready for the next body to slide into the tomb space above it. Now, with the advent of embalming and metal caskets the remains are removed (one year and a day for wooden caskets, ten years and a day for metal caskets) because those remains do not completely decompose.

The bodies are then disinterred after these time frames, regardless of the state of decomposition, and placed in a body bag. That bag either gets returned to the pit under the tomb or it is put into the coffin of the next burial into that tomb, if there is one taking place at that time. This all happen away from the view of the public or family.

The whole culture of burial in New Orleans has been built around these old traditions but they are not working anymore – this newer process of bagging and reinterring older remains is designed to make it appear at the time of a burial when family is present, that nothing has changed.

Many New Orleans cemeteries also house 'coping plots'. This is the name for a normal vault-free, in-ground burial plot that looks like a garden with a border around it. It is generally thought that these coping graves have a vault under them, but they most do not. Bodies will decompose in them, in the earth – below ground burial has always happened in New Orleans.

Vaults are a cemetery requirement, not a legal requirement. Brooke has seen a body that has decomposed in five years in the ground, even buried in a coffin. Some cemeteries have more in-ground burial than others, for example Holt Cemetery is mostly in-ground burials with wooden headstones. This cemetery is used largely by low income families. New Orleans also has a 'potter's field' (a graveyard for unclaimed or unidentified bodies). The current potter's field was established in 1967.

A lot of the city of New Orleans is below sea level however there are also parts of the city which sit five to 12 feet above sea level. The areas closer to the Mississippi River are generally those higher than sea level. The mighty

Mississippi River flows through the city and the country. It is the third longest river in the world.

There is a massive lake just outside New Orleans and when the river starts to run too high they open the levees and use their spillways to get water into the lake, avoiding a flood in the city. You don't have to go too far to see sandbags in various places around the city at any time of the year. In talking to people who have lived for a long time in New Orleans, I was told that when building new structures, it is a requirement to sink poles that are 15 to 20 feet long into the ground and they must put chains around them. Then they put in the piers and pour the concrete so that the house itself, when built, will rest on the poles, not the ground. All of this because of how far below sea level the ground is, in and around New Orleans.

It is also one of the reasons why Hurricane Katrina was so devastating when it hit New Orleans. There is a famous photo that made mainstream media during the aftermath of Katrina – a picture of a man in a canoe gathering up caskets floating in the flood waters. Brooke explained that it has been largely thought that these were the caskets buried in the ground, which had risen above the ground due to the force of the water and floated off, but the truth is actually very different. These caskets were instead the ones that had been made of metal and sealed airtight, then buried in vaults or interred in above-ground crypts. These vaults and crypts had filled with water and the water pressure on the doors has burst them open, with the caskets then floating out. Both wood and metal caskets floated out if they had not decomposed enough to get waterlogged. The more decomposed wooden coffins buried in the earth actually stayed in place.

Above-ground burials came to New Orleans as a Parisian fad – New Orleans has a large a French influence and that kind of burial was the style of the time. It was a choice that has nothing to do with the sea level; burials are not done this way due to the water table, the sea level or any other environmental concern.

There is a level of infamy about the historic cemeteries in New Orleans. There are several famous people and many urban legends around vampires and voodoo practitioners who have been immortalised in song, film and print in decades past. Because of this, tourists are getting in the way of the cemetery function and people's actual funeral processions and burials. Tomb owners feel they cannot have adequate access to their tomb site and the idea of having a

From top: Graves in Lafayette No. 2 Cemetery; Graves in St Joseph's Cemetery, New Orleans, USA

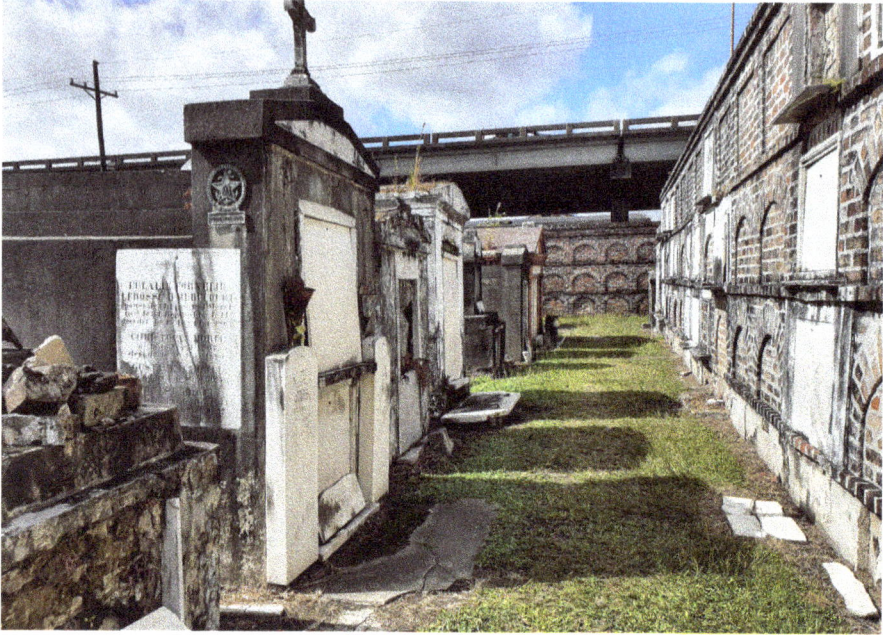

Graves in St Louis Cemetery No. 2, New Orleans, USA

place to go to remember their loved one reverently has gone for them because there are always tourists everywhere.

Even with all this publicity and infamy, many of the tombs are in varying states of decay. There is so much history contained in the tombs in New Orleans about the society, historical events and stonemasons. The owners of the cemeteries are for the most part religious institutions like various church dioceses or large funeral companies, and they are letting these tombs crumble without doing much at all to locate the family of the people buried there. Instead, they let them cave in and then when it has crumbled they re-sell the plot. Families who try to establish their lineage to take control of the family tomb find it very difficult to prove the ownership; there are very few surviving records.

There are very few support services in the city to help people connect to the tombs either, the various owners are not doing the upkeep that some think they should. They do perform basic groundskeeping but they have been known to not use proper preservation techniques and that can cause more harm to the tombs in the long run. Some private individuals are now stepping in to assist families by tracing histories of the tombs. Others are helping with restoration to their original state and colour when the owners have painted everything white.

Increasingly, people will choose cremation because it is simpler and cheaper. Those remains are still interred on consecrated ground as per the Catholic belief. The Catholic Church in New Orleans have only recently had a meeting to say that while they should encourage people to bury cremains on consecrated ground, they cannot control it or deny Catholic rites and services to those families if they want to bring the ashes home. Having said that, in New Orleans it is considered a cultural taboo, having ashes at home, even among the irreligious. Societal pressure means that people are very hush-hush about it if they do have ashes at home.

According to Brooke, funeral homes in New Orleans are still mostly divided along cultural lines: those that serve the Caucasian communities are largely Catholic and mostly corporate owned, while the ones that serve the African-American communities are largely Baptist and more local/family owned. While all funeral homes are willing and would gladly serve any family or any cultural requirement, families and communities tend to stay with the businesses that culturally understand them and can easily provide the services they want.

The African-American community have engaging services, a lot of music and they have huge public displays of grief. It is more acceptable to express their grief publicly there than in other cultures and this can often be seen through their cultural practice of jazz funerals. These are celebratory in nature, influenced by the culture of close-knit community that has existed there for a very long time. The taboo around death exists because they do not engage with death before it happens, but they do celebrate the life of a person when it does.

New Orleans has an increasing Vietnamese society, and culturally they are also hands-on with their grief and very public in their displays of emotion. By contrast, the emotional experience among French Catholics is very restrained – they don't want to be seen crying or in public displays of emotion. Grief for them is much more individual and private.

Even though death is a publicly celebrated thing, it is still taboo to talk about death. Dying and death elicit fear, and there is very little socially-created space for having conversations about it. Death in New Orleans is presented in pop culture and also historically as having a close relationship with the inhabitants. It has set the scene for many fictions in print and screen which have displayed an often symbiotic relationship between death and life. It does not take many questions with local people to get the distinct message that this is very much a thing of tourism – the fantasy of New Orleans has become its own monster. The city is not the metropolis where residents are hanging out in cemeteries and talking about their own mortality. Many locals feel that the reverence for historic cemeteries has been trampled, and the tour guides exploit and perpetuate this by telling lies and half-truths to the throng of tourists to satisfy sensationalist desires.

It is perhaps unsurprising that in Louisiana there is a 'boy's club' of sorts. The funeral industry has historically been tied to a male-dominated religion and government, however for the funeral industry this is changing. Funeral education programs are now often full of females who do not have family ties to the industry; they have chosen this as a career path and not because it was the family business.

When it comes to indigent funerals (what would once have been called paupers' funerals), the homeless are taken care of. If their families cannot find a funeral home to make a deal with for payment, then the parish will do a cremation or burial in their potter's field. The coroner has custody of the body in that time and they must do a thorough investigation of who the family of the deceased is.

Brooke and her employer operate in good faith with families in need; they discount as required and allow people to pay by instalments. The coroner's office has a storage fee so if a family has tight financial limits they will try to get the body out before the family is charged the fee.

When people think about New Orleans the imagery is often around a rich culture of voodoo, a darker side of life, a place where the unusual is coveted and accepted, and a place to party. In part this is true, but much of it has come from outside influences. The people of New Orleans celebrate life but they are just as disconnected from death as much of the rest of the USA. There is a mythology around death that brings tourists to New Orleans by the thousands, but very little of it corresponds to the lived experiences of the locals. Graves are seen in disrepair, cremation rates are on the rise and death is in the hands of institutions and industry. New Orleans has a close relationship to death in the public eye but as a community, the actual capacity to deal with death is sadly missing.

Dias de los Muertos is not celebrated all over Mexico, only in the places where the indigenous (Zapotec, Aztec, Mayan etc.) people live. While it has been appropriated by the western world and tied into Halloween, Dias de los Muertos is actually a deeply religious, cultural tradition that is centuries old and based around a firm set of values and beliefs.

Because of the large mountain range that has guarded and protected the city for centuries, Oaxaca was not so completely absorbed by the Spanish Conquest as other places in Mexico, and many of the native languages and traditions still thrive here.

While the Spanish, as a tool of conquering, destroyed many of the old temples and built churches on top, the indigenous people continued to visit the sites as they considered that the sites were still locations of great power, no matter what was built there. Some indigenous people converted to Catholicism, some did not, but over the years Catholicism has become a strong faith across the country. It exists alongside the ancient traditions and beliefs and they have melded together.

The majority of the cemeteries or the *ofrendas* (altars) made on the street, have some kind of Catholic iconography woven into them. When I spoke to people it was clear that for some, these older traditions were simply a part of their Catholic faith and for others, they were something very different – in neither case did anyone see a conflict.

In Mexico there is a very different kind of Catholicism that blends and incorporates these ancient traditions and it is different from person to person how they see this. It feels like a tradition that has been built on centuries of compromise in a place where a conquest did not entirely succeed. In villages such as Teotitlan del Valle the church was rendered over and again to cover the ancient symbols but recent work where the render has been worn down

Above: The Day of the Dead Market in Teotitlan de Valle, Oaxaca, Mexico

Left: Temple stones exposed in the outside walls of a church in Teotitlan del Valle, Mexico

has revealed the carvings on the original stones from the Zapotec temple – carvings that are thousands of years old. They are now visible for the first time on the walls of the church, and they are being left that way.

The indigenous peoples from the region of Oaxaca are the Zapotec and within that indigenous community there are many different language groups. The communities that I visited around Oaxaca are all locally run. In 1995 the Mexican government acknowledged the indigenous governance of the local communities. This means that the villages are run by a council made up of indigenous men. Some communities have progressed to the point where they do offer a small role for a woman, whose job it is to represent women's affairs, but this is not common in many communities.

Each year the leadership changes and the governing council assign jobs (called *cargos*). *Cargos* are mandatory, unpaid and in line with public service: anything from the weekly upkeep of the flowers in the church, to the maintenance of the schools, or the local police/security. *Cargos* usually go for 12 months but it is possible for them to go for up to three years. The man of the house is the one responsible for carrying them out, however in the case of single women or those divorced or widowed, women will receive *cargos* as well. This system of self-governance is in place of taxes in the communities and there are fines and consequences for a person who does not carry out their duties.

In every home, families have *ofrendas* all year round. Here they pay homage to the saints and the various connections to the Catholic faith. When Dias de los Muertos begins, the *ofrendas* are decorated and laid out in a very specific way. There are seven tiers to an *ofrenda* for Dias de los Muertos and while this varies a little from community to community the basic premises are the same.

Level 1 represents God, level 2 the saints; level 3 has salt (helps with purification of souls and offerings), level 4 has food including *pana muertos* (which is bread made with egg and butter and cardamom – or cinnamon – and only made at this time of year) and traditional handmade chocolate, as well as the various favourite foods of the deceased.

Level 5 has photographs or where there are none, then things that represent the deceased and were important to them.

Level 6 is decorated with marigolds and the other seasonal flowers, especially *Flores de Muertos* which grows wild in the mountains and on the flat. It has

An altar for Dias de los Muertos in a home in the Village San Miguel del Valle, Mexico

a very distinct smell which they say is the smell of Dias de los Muertos and families are responsible for going out each year and cutting their own supply of these branches for the altars.

Level 7 has candles, *mescal* (alcohol, usually homemade) and *copal* (incense) and other gifts and offerings.

Many of the homes in rural villages will have these things in fewer tiers but all of these items will be present. *Mescal* is often poured on the floor and parts of the *ofrenda* as an offering and a blessing each day as well. Over the altar or at the sides is sugar cane, often made in the shape of an arch, which is something sweet to welcome the ancestors.

When visiting a family during this time – and there are many visits as it is customary to visit the *ofrendas* for those people you have known who have died – it is polite to bring an offering. There are seven offerings that people can choose from: nuts, *pana muertos*, flowers, chocolate, candles, *copal* and fruit. In return for the gifts from visitors it is traditional at this time of year that every guest to a home is treated with a drink of *mescal*. The traditional food for this time of the year is *mole*, (pronounced mol-ay) and a thick hot chocolate served with *pana muertos*.

Although the celebrations are weeklong, there are three stages and three days of this celebration. There is the time of preparation for the arrival of the ancestors, the time of their arrival and the celebration with them, and then the time of their departure. These are 31 October, 1 November and 2 November respectively. It is worth noting that the ancestors of children also visit through this time, although the days are slightly different– they arrive on the day of preparation and leave the following day before the adult ancestors come.

Ofrendas can be made to one person or many. They are usually done in family groups – for example in the homes I visited the *ofrenda* was for the husband's family, and the wife's family were remembered either in their mother's or brother's home.

I was told that there are a few people who still make *ofrendas* without the actual belief in the ancestors return however I did not encounter any. All of the people I spoke to held a very firm belief that their ancestors would indeed return. A couple who I met in a cemetery cleaning the grave of their baby on 30 October, continue this tradition and spend time with that child, even though they went on to have two more children who have since both grown to adults. Together they look forward to this time with their child each year.

There are many stories both in the city and the villages about ancestors arriving at their graves or *ofrendas* and finding no offerings and leaving very sad. There are people who have seen ancestors walking the streets with nothing but stones in their baskets. When you ask the people in the villages about the idea of ancestors visiting, they say at the exact moment of arrival there are unexplainable things that happen, like flowers moving on the *ofrenda* even though it is set up inside with no wind. There are countless stories of families who stopped creating *ofrendas* and had their crops fail the following year or things fall off the walls or shelves.

All of this is not just superstition but a firmly held belief, they are the threads woven into the fabric of their culture and they are told through stories passed down over generations, and it keeps their families and communities steadfastly committed to the traditions.

During Dias de los Muertos people pray both to and for their dead regardless of burial or cremation. They pray that they will continue to come back and they pray for them to carry messages back when they return. In the more remote villages there is only burial, but in the cities cremation is also an option.

From top: Dias de los Muertos altar in a home in Teotitlan; Grave offerings for
Dias de los Muertos in the village Teotitlan del Valle, Mexico

Some families keep the ashes of their dead in their homes, on their *ofrendas* all year round, when asked they tell me that the Catholic Church has no requirement for interment in holy ground in Mexico. This is different from many other parts of the world. Instead, they are happy for people to keep their dead with them as the connection to their dead makes people happy. The connection to the dead is lifelong.

In the city communities, before someone dies the person is given the final prayers, what we would call the last rites. When someone dies in the communities outside the city the body stays in the family home and a network is activated. People inform neighbours and friends; the bells are rung in the local church and people start to arrive.

Professional people are paid to take care of the body and they come to pray for them. Those professionals are community elders who start practising the prayers for the dead from about the age of 40 and by the time they are community elders this becomes their paid work. The body of the deceased usually stays at home for one day and one night, sometimes two. During this time friends and community members come and stay in the home with the deceased; they can travel from a long way away for this. They bring offerings for the *ofrendas* and spend time with the deceased.

Carpenters in the villages make the coffins and depending on the village, there are people who dig graves or groups of men in the family unit who do the digging. The body is placed in a coffin when it arrives and then after the initial day and night, the family transports the coffin to the church for a mass and then to the cemetery for burial. This all happens quickly.

During the day and night at home and on the journey to the graveyard the family maintain a very intense conversation with the dead. They talk to their dead, they give them messages and they say all the things that may have been unsaid in life. In some cases, they are so stricken with grief that they do not get to say all that they wanted to and so times like Dias de los Muertos mean that they can then have that opportunity again, even if they must wait many months for it.

The recently dead do not come to the next Dias de los Muertos that follows their death, their first visit is the following one. This seems to have something to do with the process of ancestors returning and leaving again and having time to detach before the visit.

Flower stall for traditional Dias de los Muertos flowers, Oaxaca, Mexico

Catholics believe in Purgatory, where a soul can be trapped and not reach its proper destination, and so often prayers can revolve around the safe journey of the soul to that final destination.

Marigolds and *copal* are used all through the funeral processions from the home to the church and the graveyard; salt is also used for its purification properties. These things are seen as the link, or the bridge, from the other side to this. Musicians lead the procession – in the villages they play from the family home all the way to the church and the graveyard. Everyone is present for a series of prayers at home before the procession and the prayers and conversations with the dead continue throughout the travels to the church.

Perhaps because it is such a short time between death and burial, there are rituals around aftercare for the family of the deceased as well. It is customary in the villages to gather at the family home and proceed to the grave 9 days after burial, again after 40 days and finally on the year anniversary. These gatherings

Stall selling copal used on altars during Dias de los Muertos, Oaxaca, Mexico

are a comfort and support to the families. It is also one of the ways to ensure that people are checking in with the bereaved family and looking after them.

In the villages it is also common that people go every week to the cemetery. They take fresh flowers and spend time in contemplation of their dead. This is yet another of the ways that they keep their memory of their dead alive and stay connected to them and during Dias de los Muertos they get to visit with them as well.

No one is gone forever unless they are forgotten.

This idea of not forgetting is alive in the city as well, however not always to the same extent – the cemeteries are visited with less frequency through the year for some people. Others choose cremation and so they remain connected with the ashes at home. In the cities the more traditional families can choose to have the body at home but more commonly the body is taken to a funeral home and the family go there to sit vigil with their dead for the 24 hours before the mass and burial or cremation. Some funeral homes do not allow overnight visitation and so the families stay for as long as they can and are there at opening time the next morning. In Mexico City I was told that cremation is more common than burial; space is an issue but so is cost.

Mexico City rests in what was the Aztec region of Mexico and in that region there are no times prescribed for the arrival or departure of the ancestors. There are simply the known as the days or arrival, celebration and departure in the Dias de los Muertos festival and they are treated accordingly. Even in the bustle of Mexico City, I found a firm belief that the ancestors do indeed come back and visit.

The *ofrenda* decorations for Dias de los Muertos in the family home and the decoration of the graves stay for a week. Mexicans believe that it is important not to take the decorations down or the offerings away too quickly. The families, after a week, will use what they can of what is left on the *ofrenda*, the bread and any fruit etc. Nothing is simply discarded unless it is no longer able to be used.

One question I asked most people was around the idea of grief and if the time of Dias de los Muertos made grief easier in any way when a person died. Overwhelmingly, the answer was yes. While the first Dias de los Muertos is very hard, they look forward to the opportunity to spend time with their dead; they see it as a sacred time. Yet they still feel grief. One woman I spoke to talked about losing the will to live when her daughter died, but over time and with the support of family and friends as well as the tradition of Dias de los Muertos, she came to see the benefit of living on, maintaining the close contact with the dead. She has her daughter's ashes with her on her *ofrenda*, and she now feels that she can maintain a meaningful kind of closeness.

The day of preparation is one loaded with excitement for families. There are pop-up markets everywhere selling all the wares for an *ofrenda* and many of the things considered as good offerings as well. The market is a hive of activity and there's an air of expectation for the times to come. In the villages there are specific times assigned to the arrival of ancestors. In San Miguel del Valle it is midday, in Teotitlan del Valle it is 3pm.

Family sharing story
and song at the grave
of their ancestors,
Oaxaca, Mexico

Artist installation of Catrina figures in Oaxaca, Mexico

In both those villages at the designated times there are fireworks (homemade), music and all kinds of noise to welcome the ancestors. People gather at their *ofrendas*. They burn *copal* and share memories and time together. Some choose to gather at the cemetery, others go there in the evenings. These gatherings are for families to share stories and memories of the deceased; they sing songs and pay their respects. Friends come and honour their deceased as well. Some of the songs that are sung are from the perspective of the deceased. It is a beautiful giving and receiving.

At night on the day of celebration, I wandered around the big general cemetery in Oaxaca. There were movie screenings, bands and such a celebratory atmosphere with street parties and sideshow alley-style events. There were families around their graves, telling stories of their dead and singing many beautiful songs. It is both a symbolic and a tangible time of sharing and connection. It was slightly marred by the several (dare I say it, arrogant) tourists who were drinking and cavorting in a manner that could not be considered respectful, but it did not seem to dampen the beautiful and authentic family times going on off the beaten track, which is where I wanted to spend my time. One beautiful family I spoke to allowed me to take a photo and in return I left an offering for their grave.

Someone described Dias de los Muertos to me as a serious celebration, which seems quite apt. As fun and party-like as it can be, there's a deep, rich connection to the dead and everything here is for a reason.

The final day, the day of farewell, can be difficult. For those who have recently experienced the death of loved ones, they know it will not be until the following year that they will visit, so they wait. The time for farewell lacks the celebratory atmosphere of the day before and it is also remarkably different in the graveyards away from the city and the masses of tourists.

I spent time with a family who run a café and weaving business and their grandma makes chocolate for sale. We ate with them, gave offering to their *ofrenda* and then at the cemetery after dark one of the owners took me to her mother's grave and shared with me her experiences with death: the ritual, the practice and her own experiences when her mother died. She took me to the church where we sat listening to a group of men singing *cantos*, which are like funeral songs, songs for the dead. It was quite unique. So many families were huddled together around the individual graves saying their own goodbyes. There was a beautiful sense of community and this was reinforced through the year in how the community responded when one of their community members died. Mexico, for all its differences, lives the community capacity the West is trying to build.

The notion of the *Catrinas* (the skeleton faces) has a long and layered history. It is common to see people with variations of skeletons painted on their faces as they parade through the streets – and parades and music, food and festivities are common and numerous wherever Dias de los Muertos is celebrated, city or country. Many tourists think it is as a reminder of death and mortality and a celebration of the ancestors. And perhaps this is what it has come to represent, however it is actually an incredibly deeper and more political statement.

Women dressed as *Catrinas* in the parade on the *day of preparation*, Oaxaca, Mexico

The first *Catrina* was created as only a skull, an unnamed papier-mâché head. Artist Jose Gudalupe Posada created it as a statement of defiance and disgust at his people having been denied their culture and heritage ever since the Spanish Conquest. Many wealthier Mexicans had taken on the European influence in style and dress and he felt that this was a kind of 'selling out'. This was in the early 1900s and after that, the artist Diego Rivera gave the face a skeleton body and the finery from Europe, including the fancy hat and the snake figure. This became an incredibly powerful and visible political statement of the appropriation and wealth of Europe profiting on the backs of the Mexican heritage. He also coined the term '*Catrina*': a slang word for 'rich'.

The parades of people with their faces painted in this way is more than a tribute to the dead. It is a defiant act of reclaiming the culture and history stripped from the indigenous peoples.

CONCLUSION

Human bones on display in Sedlec Ossuary, a Roman Catholic Chapel found below the
Cemetery Church of All Saints in Sedlec, Kutna Hora, Czech Republic

A walking track through the Ramsey Creek Burial Ground, South Carolina, USA

Many people are talking about what happens before death. As a society, we have started to get reasonably good at things like Wills, Powers of Attorney, Enduring Guardianship, Advance Care Directives; or at least we are starting to get good at talking about them. Agency and capacity for the ageing and the dying is much more present now than it used to be, but there is still a long way to go.

But I found myself asking, what about after death? Sure, if we have a Will, we have an Executor to make decisions, but comparatively little thought is given to what will happen to our bodies beyond cremation or contemporary burial. The result of this is an ill-informed public, largely unaware of the choices available to them, who are then thrust into a cycle of death care and ceremony that may or may not benefit them emotionally and may burden them financially.

In the last 120 years we have lost over 5000 years of knowledge about caring for our dead, but times are again changing. Ways are emerging around the world to both challenge and change how we in the West currently approach dying and death. It is more than paperwork and planning, although they are both necessary components. Within these approaches, people are finding ways of reframing death from a negative experience into one where people can discover a kind of sovereignty in their mortality. We are reclaiming our own social narratives and leaning into the 'taboo' of death to discover new ways to connect with each other.

What needs to happen now is a focus on the bigger picture.

At present, there are many different approaches to ceremony and body disposal, and hundreds of people are working worldwide in their communities to educate and increase death literacy and introduce methods of community capacity; but they are all working individually. By coming together, there is the option of creating a greater force, a louder voice, and to do this there needs to be unity in the messages being given to the public. This unity starts with agreeing on the language to be used, and the boundaries and scope of the roles to be performed in this space. This begins by defining what we call the roles and the work in the end-of-life space.

At present, credibility in this end-of-life work is largely found in the experiences with death that call us to it. And this is incredibly valid – stories are one of the most underrated forms of education in the modern western world. Doctors, academics and lay people alike – all relate to each other through lived experience in addition to their learning and skill.

While there are those who question the validity of the non-medical role of doula becoming a profession, it appears that the role is indeed heading that way and there is an inherent shared responsibility in this space to respond appropriately. We must not lose focus on why this work exists: to provide agency and build capacity within families to achieve better grief and bereavement outcomes and with the dying to provide better deaths.

Given the large number of individuals who go through versions of training each year, there is also a responsibility that needs to be borne by the trainers themselves, both in Australia and overseas, to actively work towards and seek out a sustainable market for their graduates to enter. There is work to be done in creating the space for this paid work in all its various forms, including within the medical and care facilities. This could be as an additional kind of complimentary or allied health therapy. Once a doula is paid for their work, they can choose when to give their service away to those in need and as a service-based and service-driven role. This is hopefully and I believe a likely, outcome.

It needs to be acknowledged that almost no one is working full-time as a doula yet, earning a full-time living. I did not encounter anyone, anywhere I travelled, earning a full-time living unless they were paid employees of another end-of-life service such as a hospice, or they were providing training to do this work. In this way, the role of the doula at the moment is largely a labour of love and driven by a desire to help others. Currently, doulas and death care advocates are the front line for community education worldwide and the support for them and the need for their services is still being established in the end-of-life space.

There is a need to unite the voices and the ideas developing in the western world, under one resource that can be a platform for the community education for all the paths that are a part of this growing movement. A single message would create a more powerful move towards change and acceptance. As I mentioned, I have discovered that many people are all reinventing the wheel in their own little corner of the world and wondering why it is like pushing honey up a hill.

If there were to emerge a united network of voices, education would become much easier, as would acceptance and then engagement of the services. This is a pattern seen throughout history where real change is effected when grassroots-style social justice movements have come together to become a strong, global voice pushing for a reclaiming of autonomy where it has otherwise been found lacking. This is precisely what the current end-of-life and death movement is aiming for.

This must be done in a compelling way. Many people have tried before but have not presented the topic of death in an elegant or appealing way such as is needed to garner people's interest and engagement. Death is a hot topic when it is abstract; remind someone they or someone they care for is actually going to die and it becomes less so. Currently it is the people and groups that have captured the public with their stories, their vulnerability and their honesty about death, that have built the largest public following. These more recent brands, built around various personalities, have also created a platform that has allowed the conversation about options at the end of life to have a wider audience than ever before.

It is with this spread of influence that doors are beginning to open, allowing for the diverse developments explored in this research. While these disruptive technologies, people and approaches, have been largely born of grassroots-

Bec and Dr Pia Interlandi, 2019 National Home Funeral Alliance Conference, Minnesota, USA

style lived experience, they have gained traction through the stories that have accompanied them; the public attention this space is receiving is steadily growing.

This attention has been two-fold. On the one hand it has looked at agency at the end of life, the decisions around how people want to die, where and under what circumstances. This conversation came first and is better understood now, but more recently there has been an increased interest in agency after death as well, in relation both to ceremony and body disposal. In this way it seems the options are expanding just as fast as the public platform for their understanding and acceptance is. Much of this seems to be driven by the desire to find and fund greener methods of body care and disposal.

The move towards greener approaches to the end of life has acknowledged that both cremation and contemporary burial do harm rather than good to the earth and people are increasingly seeking a better way to dispose of our mortal remains. People are also seeking agency over that choice. There are various options now on offer, others still being trialled and even more still being developed as theories. Under scrutiny, some of these are no better than contemporary methods, while some may even be worse from an environmental standpoint. That remains to be seen – but from all of these options, the conversations have begun.

Within this environmental approach are the considerations around authenticity and integrity. While there are demands being made of the service providers to operate with these high moral, social and ecological benchmarks, there is also the reality of navigating the preferencing of a family's emotional consideration over the integrity of the eco-requirements. While there is undoubtedly a move towards greener methods of disposal from the public's point of view, there is also a kind of compromising from the movement itself, putting the grief and bereavement outcome for the family ahead of the requirements of disposal.

A good example of this is the acceptance of an embalmed body in a natural burial ground to honour the wishes of a deceased who happened to die outside the country and was required to be embalmed for repatriation. These kinds of compromises require careful consideration and much more discussion.

Financial constraints and the rising cost of death have been behind a push for more affordable options at the end of life as well. Access to ritual and ceremony for those who are grieving and bereaved is for some an equity issue which can call into question the validation of the relationship that they are mourning. The current social move away from ritual and ceremony for financial reasons, robs people of the only framework society provides them with to move into their grief and through it. As Caitlin Dougherty pointed out, current funeral practices give the family only one job – to grieve, but they offer no clear action or task to express that grief.

Many believe that touch and the hands-on care for the dead to be of vital importance in the process of grieving. It is the action of care-giving that forms the basis for the expressions of grief, the process of letting go and ultimately the gentle movement into bereavement. So many times, people told me about the differences they witnessed in families, as they were able to spend time with the body of their person, to touch them and come to terms in their own time with the state of lifelessness before them.

Australia is not without its advocates in this space. There is perhaps no bigger advocate for this than Dr Pia Interlandi who has spent many years helping people move into bereavement through touch and knows firsthand the healing that can accompany it. She spends part of her time speaking about this through

An urn containing Frida Kahlo's ashes in the *Blue House*, Frida Khalo Museum, Mexico

her own personal experiences and helping families have their own. This healing difference seen in the families is talked about and written about often. It is the subject of much of the storytelling we have about this kind of end-of-life care and it is beginning to form part of the death narrative that we as a society are reclaiming.

When we spoke at the NHFA Conference in Minnesota, Dr Interlandi also reminded me that without the stories, we as a society run the risk of overlooking the practical application of the theoretical insights of all this academic study. Academics are beginning to delve into this end-of-life space both in the dying and after-death approaches, looking at what kind of response can be made to the public push for difference in service, considering the increasing rates of death predicted. They are not easily reconciled.

It is clear that we need further and urgent academic study. It has a vital place, and yet it is only part of the picture. The actions of death care performed by families and their engagement with the non-academic, non-medical service providers and the various grassroots approaches are all equally part of a broader conversation, and that is where all the research becomes real. Families are less concerned with the studies behind why something is, and more concerned with how it feels – they are concerned with their grief, ritual and journey. To this end, what needs to be looked at closely is the anecdotal benefits that form the storytelling narrative we have around these new end-of-life approaches.

One thing that is widely agreed on is that there is a wave of death coming. Put simply, we do not have the doctors, nurses, palliative care wards, places in nursing homes, aged care workers, hospice programs, hospital beds, funeral homes etc. to deal with the numbers of people who are projected to die in the next four decades. Radical and innovative thinking about dying and death and the infrastructure needed to cope with the projected death rate is essential if we are to ensure the best possible outcomes for the dying and their families.

As a society we are ill equipped to cope with the death rates that we are going to see in coming years. It is inevitable that something must change, and the hope is that the community, along with emerging roles such as doulas, will need to step in to fill the gaps that are already opening up. This is the point of ventures like Compassionate Communities – skilling people to look after people, acknowledging that death belongs to the community and social groups of the dying.

What cannot be forgotten in all of this is that the central idea of this movement, this reclaiming, is to increase the community's and the family's capacity to care for their own. To give them the agency of choice where it has been systematically stripped away by the development of contemporary living in the western world.

As much as we are seeing the emergence of new roles at the end of life, and as much as they have a very valid place in the space, the ultimate goal should always be the support of families to do things themselves. This means that by skilling and educating communities and families, locally and globally, their levels of death literacy increase and they have agency in a full range of choices available to them.

Ultimately, the goal is for people to feel empowered to do things for themselves and that should they choose to engage any kind of service at all, for it to be an informed choice born of considered thought rather than necessity.

MY FELLOWSHIP RECOMMENDATIONS

- More focus should be placed on end-user outcomes (the family's experience) in the research that is being done into body disposal technologies.

- There needs to be more research to look at the science behind the vast anecdotal evidence showing that the acts of being in contact with, and care-giving for, the dead, make for improved and healthier grief and bereavement outcomes.

- Specific research is required into the effects on the soil and organisms within the soil that surrounds the buried bodies that have been embalmed, had temporary preservation done, and those that contain foreign objects such as pacemakers, to contribute to current conversations around integrity of the burial vs. a family's emotional need.

- Very clear boundaries need to be set around the definition of and roles of a doula both globally and in Australia.

- Introduction of micro-credentialing and proficiency accreditations. They have a limited place within this end-of-life work and introducing this in Australia will mean that a national standard will be created for doula training.

- Medical communities and facilities need to implement doula-led educational strategies within their organisations with the view to adopt the doula role into paid positions as non-medical support – they should be an addition to the staff of every hospital and care facility. This should be promoted through partnerships with organisations such as Palliative Care Australia.

- Experienced doulas should be included in the teaching of courses for nurses and doctors in relation to their awareness and understanding of this role as a complimentary therapy. (Currently other complimentary therapies have the opportunity to present in this context in various programs.)

- The Australian, American, Canadian and British Governments need to fund a global summit for all the stakeholders in this movement to come together and formulate direction and responses to issues and situations such as those identified in this research and listed below:
  - A need to ascertain agreement on language
  - Standardise micro-credentialing if it is to be standard

- Formulate a response and plan for future development while not falling into cultural appropriation
- Response to the 'silver tsunami'
- Opportunity to create a global network and what that will look like
- Find direction and ways of ensuring inclusivity
- Defining doula and the boundaries of the role and the work
- Strategies for building bridges with medical-based stakeholders and other service providers within the bio-medical models.

- There needs to be infrastructure developed in Australia that can govern, plan and direct these new end-of-life services. Establish membership-based organisations and/or a peak body to hold the standards for practice and manage the credentialing.

- A Foundation Charity should be established to fund those who are in marginalised communities to receive the training and be able to better serve their communities.

- Educational courses should be established and offered within the funeral industry, potentially through peak body conferences and seminars to provide learning to the contemporary directors on the value and space that the doula role holds for families at the end of life. From these, partnerships can be built to encourage end-of-life professionals to work together towards better end-of-life outcomes for community.

- A death literacy course should be developed for implementation across Australia. This could be provided as a free service under a government health initiative with a commitment to increasing death literacy outcomes for Australians.

- Advance Care Planning has an item number in Australia; after-death planning needs to be attributed an item number as well. There needs to be the same seriousness and importance attributed to the after-death planning as there is to the dying process.

DISSEMINATION AND IMPLEMENTATION

Since my return at the end of 2019, I have been keen to start spreading the word about my findings and keen to implement some of my ideas. Covid-19 has somewhat hampered those efforts and like the rest of the world we are still navigating all the restrictions that come with living safely in a pandemic.

I have begun giving talks about my research and findings to small community groups and local ABC radio. I have done a guest lecture by Skype with Falmouth University UK and sessions on the Fellowship and end-of-life options spot at the Hobart University of the Third Age and Specialist Palliative Care volunteers in Launceston. I was a guest presenter for the New York Death Salon and have written various pieces for public interest.

More recently, I have developed a series of workshops beginning in Tasmania looking at the various facets of the broad death conversation, developed and presented a 5-hour CPD (continuing professional development) session for nurses to be delivered through HERC (Health Education Resource Centre) training, which I am pleased to say is an ongoing engagement. I have also recently presented at the 2021 Australian Independent Funeral Professionals Conference.

In 2020 I was elected the President of the Natural Death Advocacy Network (NDAN) www.ndan.com.au and over the preceding 12 months was able to introduce to our NDAN community and the wider Australian public, many of the people and services I encountered on my Fellowship.

Most importantly, I came back from the Fellowship with the fervent belief that it was time to establish a peak body in Australia that can work alongside the international organisations such as the UK Home Funeral Network, National Home Funeral Alliance or the National End of Life Doula Alliance in the USA. This was something I had spoken to many people about and was adamant that we needed to unite to gain traction in this space. A peak body could give a national profile as well as work at defining the roles and work that is being offered in Australia, providing a national platform for referral and education. To this end I gathered a group of willing and generous experts to start what we now call the Australian Home Funeral Alliance. www.ahfa.org.au. Still in its infancy, there is a long and I hope fruitful, road ahead.

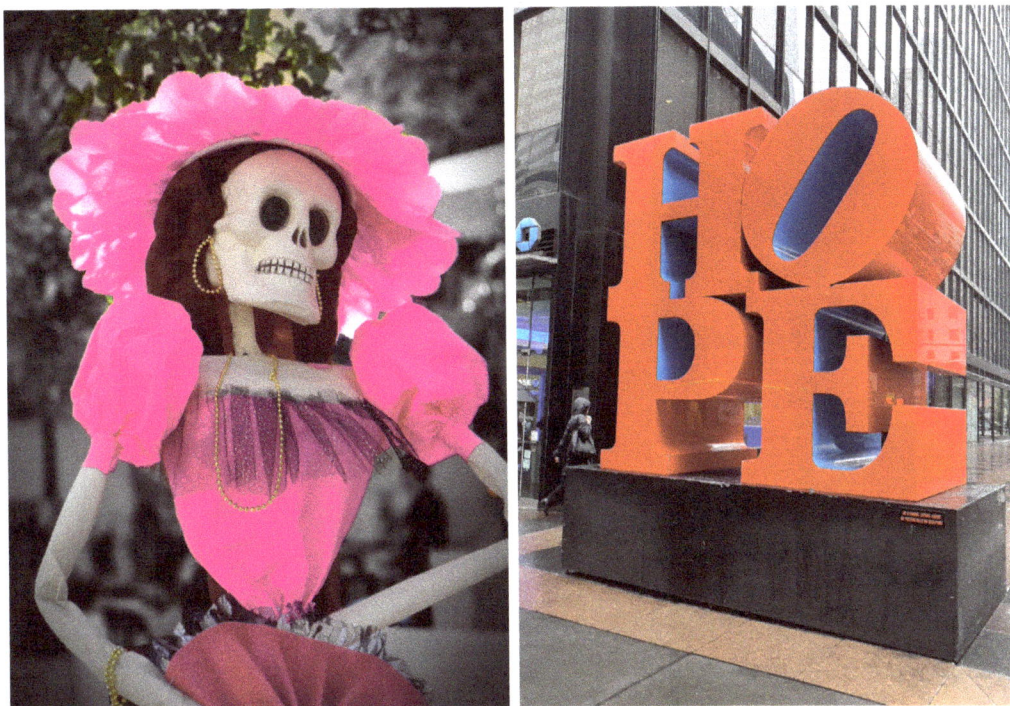

From left: A large *Catrina*, part of a street art installation during Dias de los Muertos in Oaxaca, Mexico; a street art installation, 'Hope', New York City, USA

Finally, one of the long term goals I hold is to work towards a global summit, where those at the non-medical front line of end-of-life care can bring to the table strategies, ideas and planning to formulate a response to compliment those medical responses being sought to the current death rates that are predicted. This summit would also provide an opportunity for an international conversation on many other important fronts as well. It would allow for huge input and global clarity around the definitions and roles in as far as they can apply internationally, and also for establishing partnerships and a global platform for the public education and advocacy going forward.

I hope that one day the words 'doula' and 'home funeral' are as commonly understood and widely known and used as the words 'palliative care' and 'hospice.'

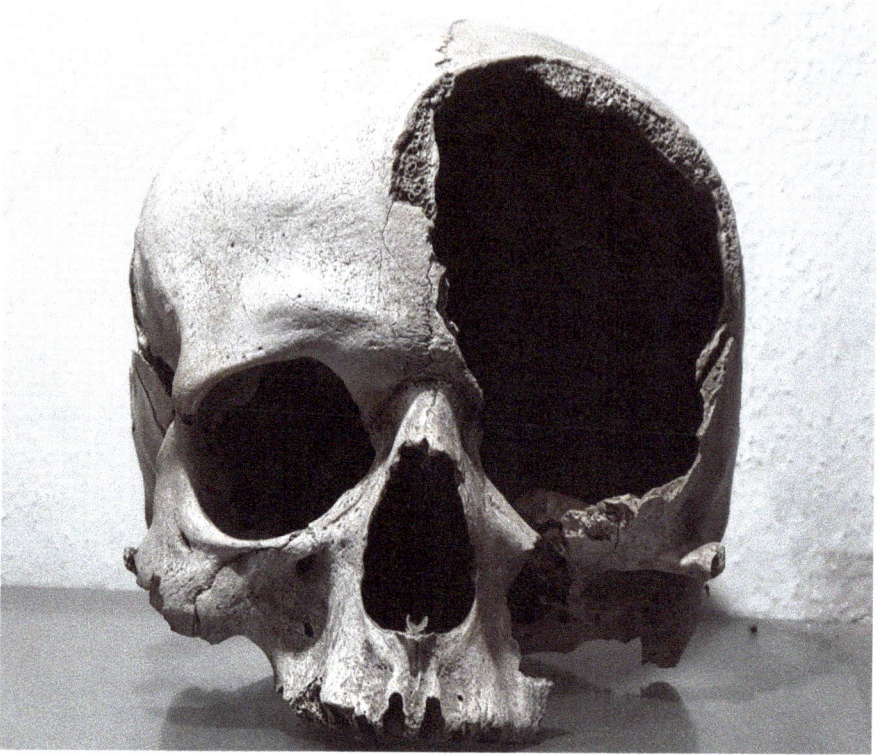

Skulls on display in Sedlec Ossuary, a Roman Catholic Chapel found below the
Cemetery Church of All Saints in Sedlec, Kutna Hora, Czech Republic

The seats set before Judy Garland's crypt, Hollywood Forever Cemetery,
Los Angeles, USA

CRITICAL ISSUES
FOR FURTHER CONSIDERATION

Throughout this research there were themes and issues identified which require further thought and conversation. What I offer here are my own opinions, thoughts and learnings; this is a changing landscape and as such, end-of-life care in Australia and across the globe would benefit from a public dialogue on these things.

LANGUAGE OF DEATH

I have always been fascinated by the language of death: the words we choose to associate with the state of being or becoming dead. The fact that how we talk about something frames how we experience it could not be clearer when considering death, nor could it be more important in the movement to reclaim agency in the death care process.

The language that we use around death is designed to disconnect us from the reality of the one common thing that we all share: our mortality. There is very little surer in life than the fact that we will all eventually die, and before that there is every likelihood that we will have to deal with the death of someone we love. It is a very strange thing then, that while we know this to be our human truth, as a society we have embraced a framework through which to view and discuss this inevitable event that shields us, deflects and restricts us from the agency we would otherwise have in the journey of dying and death.

In all my years in the funeral industry, these are some of the common euphemisms I have encountered to avoid the words 'dead' and 'death':

'kicked the bucket, passed away, passed on, pushing up daisies, six feet under, promoted to glory, born into eternal life, departed, gone, lost, shuffled off this mortal coil, released from suffering, left the earthly realm, flying with the angels, gone to a better place, resting in eternal peace, entered their peaceful slumber, graduated to heaven, called home, gone to the happy hunting ground in the sky, breathed his last, bid farewell to the world, didn't make it, lost the battle, gave up the ghost...'

It is an exhaustive and I am sure an incomplete list. And when it comes to dying, we do not do much better. Even doctors talk about 'care' plans and palliative 'care' often without ever explaining that the patient is in fact dying.

'Passed away peacefully' is arguably the most common and overused euphemism. Now forgetting the fact that far from all deaths are peaceful, passed away has come to represent a finality that does not actually exist in the language when you break it down. Passed – old, gone, finished; away – far, distant, over there... it is a statement that embodies the movement of something to a place separate from us, and it lacks the finality of death. It is used because it is seen as a gentler and less confronting way to express the expiration of life and instead it allows us to continue the mythology we have built around death.

The couched language of death has a hidden message, it wraps death in a form of love and kindness, so as not to offend the readers… and yet the more I speak to families, the more I see a desire for the dialogue to be honest, personal and reflective of the life (and death) of the dead.

Some people carry over this desire for honesty into what they write about the dead. It is a brave move to write a death notice that states quite plainly that someone died, but there is a raw honesty to it that seems to help people begin to look at the days and weeks ahead because the reality is that the death notice is often the first thing that family will write; before a eulogy or tribute, before they plan a funeral or ceremony, often before they have made any of the decisions they are going to be called upon to make in the time ahead.

All of the socially acceptable language of avoidance exists to mitigate the weight we attribute to the words dead and death, and yet rather than softening the blow it actually hands us a perfect avoidance strategy which we have all too readily bought into, the end result is that it perpetuates our naïvety about, and lack of agency in, end-of-life choice.

Another interesting point of severance that has occurred on a social level in relation to our language is the shift from 'him/her' and 'he/she' to 'it' and 'the body' when we talk about the dead. Even when a person discusses the death of someone they truly loved, it is remarkable how often statements such as this can be heard – 'When mum died, we didn't really know what to do. We knew she wanted to be cremated so the nurses called the funeral director and they took the body away really quickly'. There is a huge disconnect where we separate the person and the person's body. The body is spoken of as an object more than it is a person. This allows us to disassociate ourselves in a way, keeping our person as separate to the body being taken away, burned or buried. It is another layer of avoidance, and it is this avoidance which is combated through spending time with and giving hands-on care to the body of the person who has died; the power of touch has a way of connecting us with our dead like no other.

There is a further point about language when it relates to the dying. There is much talk about the idea of the war mentality in our discourse on death. We fight cancer and battle illness. We attack viruses and combat bacteria. We survive. We lose the fight. We battle our last.

The mentality around fighting cancer and other illnesses sets someone up for failure: eventually we will die of something. This language of war is a language of fear which has been handed to us and we have adopted it without question. It is a framework around how we experience illness and it goes some way to explain why doctors see death as a failure, so much is geared up to curing the ill that the idea of a good death is not seen as a successful outcome, and it should be.

Angela Ward of Go Simply Funerals in the UK held a masterclass at the Bath University conference in relation to our language and the way we use it when discussing dying and death. She highlighted that many people now are picking up on the idea of the war mentality and the expectations this language puts on the dying and their families. It is heavily weighted and burdensome dialogue.

I particularly see a problem with the idea of loss. *'I'm sorry for your loss', 'I lost my person last year.'* Really? There is a lot cloaked within that word.

When I lose my car keys, I inevitably follow with a feeling of being irresponsible, careless perhaps, and the inevitable guilt with that comes at accepting I should have been more careful with them. It's my fault. There's an inference that had more attention been paid, I would know where they were. So, when we 'lose' a person there is an implied neglect or lack of attention. Did we do enough, help enough, what if we had done something differently. It helps to feed the fear and guilt through which we view our own deaths and that of others.

We are looking at death through this biased language which is designed to distance us from it, and what it does is make us afraid and uncertain. It keeps us unquestioning; it keeps us following social convention without taking the time to consider all the options. Death is a natural process of transition from one state to another and it is a shared experience between the dying and those who will live on. There is power in the reclaiming of death and there is the opportunity for creating social cohesion and community capacity for looking after each other. We need to reframe our thinking about death and a large part of that is using the appropriate language.

But it is not just language; we can avoid death in how we treat it as well. Many people do not like to think of their own death, they feel as if they are tempting fate or they are so terrified and uncomfortable they find they are unable to negotiate their way through the necessary thoughts and decisions they will eventually be called upon to arrive at. So, we lock it away, we put it in a box, we

The space in which I gave a public talk about home funerals and the benefits of a hands-on approach to death, Prague, Czech Republic

know it is there but the longer we can go on 'living' without it, the better. Or so it seems. Death is our constant companion. It is never far away. As resilient as the human body is, it is also incredibly fragile.

DEAD. There are many reasons we should call things what they actually are.

When it comes to children, there is a necessity to have them understand the nature of death and what it means for the one who has died and for them who live on. Parents have been told for decades now in relation to children and various subjects from body parts to social situations, that a child's development will always be better if the right language is used with them from a young age. Death is no different. So many times I have heard adults talk about how they remembered experiencing the death of a relative but only from a distance and usually they were left wondering 'where is this better place grandma went, can I go there... and when will she be back?' Even in my own young childhood I was kept at home away from the death of my grandfather and his funeral – it deepened my trauma and sense of grief.

The same can be said for the disabled community. As a funeral director I experienced situations where well-meaning carers and family members came in to arrange a pre-paid or 'at need' funeral and had someone with them who required a form of disability support. Often they were unintentionally shielded, talked over, left without explanation – this can exacerbate their trauma and grief; it is unnecessary. In an effort not to upset the sensibilities of people, we can unwittingly do more harm.

Another point to note is about the sanitisation that exists within our language around death. The funeral industry is particularly good at talking about things such as temporary preservations, hygienic preparations, embalming, looking after someone's dignity... all of these procedures have a valid place in contemporary care of a deceased in a funeral home, however the language used does two basic things.

First, it disguises the actual processes that are going to take place in relation to the care of that body, things like stitching the mouth shut, packing cavities or inserting eye caps. Secondly, it reinforces to the families and the general public that death is always dirty, unsanitary and unhygienic and therefore must be carried out by a professional. Which is untrue far more than it is ever fact.

Dying, death and grief are natural things that we will all experience in our lives and it can be a healthy, albeit hard experience. It is possible to move into a healthy state of bereavement when your grief is not over-complicated or stifled by these death-avoidant language devices that are designed to separate us from it entirely.

DEATH, THE HOT TOPIC

Death is a hot topic. There are many people worldwide looking at the end of life and much is being done to put frameworks around how we as a society are going to respond to the future and likely increasing death rates. The vast majority of this is focused on the dying: how do we give people the deaths they want; how they want it to be; and where they want it to be. What medical resources are there to support those decisions and what of the people power?

Less talked about at the moment, is what will happen to all of those bodies once death occurs? We have already seen some of the projections made in relation to deaths that are expected in the decades to come, in its current state medical and funeral services would not be able to adequately deal with those volumes.

Universities and private industries are starting to fund and explore approaches. Death Tech is a group of people I met at the Bath University conference, but they are based in Melbourne University and they have the funding to study alternatives to body disposal technologies; how the technology is being used and implemented. The practical applications of these technologies is largely outside their scope (that is, how they are experienced by the families). Death Tech are tasked to and funded to follow the progress of new technologies in the space of body disposal; they received an initial funding for three years to report on and document groups/businesses starting new disposal technologies and they have met and spoken to many people including many of the people offering alkaline hydrolysis, Recompose and Promession. They are doing good and necessary work documenting the end of life space, the changes occurring and how it effects the industry and community.

The Death Tech team are doing thorough work and were keen to share their ideas and findings and welcoming of my exploration of similar issues, albeit from a vastly different point of view. More recently they have published a paper looking at the funeral industry during the Covid-19 pandemic and the lack of adequate support as essential workers they have received.

It occurred to me, upon meeting Death Tech and many of the other academics at the Centre for Death and Society conference at Bath University, that if academics are beginning to investigate and report on the 'alternative' spaces of body disposal then it is also entirely possible that similar academics may soon be studying, documenting and reporting on – but not necessarily carrying out 'the work' of – a doula, home funeral guide or family funeral practitioner/ director. In doing so, they may also begin to define both the roles, duties and concepts of the services those roles can offer.

I see potential problems with this if, as a grassroots movement, we do not maintain a voice and a say in what defines us. This is imperative in moving forward, in addition to being validated and analysed by academics and those looking at this space through an analytical lens. What we do not want are people unfamiliar with the work, placing firm definitions on it without understanding the value it has from within.

The reason for this has to do with approach – in the doing of the work we are focusing on the families not the processes: we are working to skill families and communities, to increase community capacity from the ground up, and to open people to the possibility of their being a part of the death journey of their person and thereby gaining the positively impactful grief and bereavement outcomes from doing so. None of this involves building frameworks and boundaries to define or categorise that work. The development to date has been far too organic for that.

In conversation with Dr Pia Interlandi, founder of the Australia's Natural Death Advocacy Network and creator of Interland and Garments for the Grave, Pia pointed out that not only have we not given a definitive definition to the roles at the end of life in the alternate space but we actually have not even explored and defined the scope of what 'the work' actually is. Pia, who is arguably one of the most knowledgeable people in the country in relation to the many facets of death, the transformative space around dressing our dead and disposals such as natural burial, believes this is one of the gaps yet to be filled. I have to agree.

Attempts at defining what this work is needs to be made with a holistic and broad approach, and while there may be some resistance to the inevitable constraint this defining process will put on the roles, it is the next logical step on the path to building legitimacy and carving out the space for the roles in end-of-life care. What we need to do is stake our claim, so to speak, and define the roles and services with steadfast and universally translatable frameworks and guidelines.

This will not only help with community engagement, meaning that we can start to have a solid narrative for people to learn (in the same way people tend to know what 'hospice' is regardless of who offers the actual service), but it will also mean that once defined there can be a level of both accountability and uniformity in the training and delivery of the various services.

Essentially, to have a valid seat at the table with other medical, social and complimentary services we need to have clearly defined roles and responsibilities and be accountable for the provision of reliable services with a large degree of continuity.

Death is the hot topic and we have very notable personalities bringing the conversation to a wider audience than ever before. Now that across various sectors interest is growing, and we have a flood of books, articles and writings about this space, it is time to find a universal narrative that we write for ourselves that will highlight, enhance and progress the meaningful and valuable nature of our work.

US AND THEM
– STAKEHOLDER ENGAGEMENT WITH THE FUNERAL INDUSTRY

It is important to remember that while much of the aged care and funeral industry exists in the realm of the corporate world and big business, on an individual level people generally go into the end-of-life space with the best of intentions. I have not met a funeral home employee, nurse, hospice worker or doula yet who entered the industry for the big bucks or the prestige.

Let me be clear from the outset. The industry around death, the corporatisation and the commercialisation that has been built up around dying, death and ceremony is another matter altogether and should be addressed as such. I feel it is important to separate those business models from the people who work for them – acknowledging that each of those businesses contain people who care, and most of those people have a desire to serve; many of them hold the full and complete belief that they are doing things the best way they can. There is an abundance of compassion to be found in the hearts of the employees within corporate industries and that needs to be seen and respected for what it is. Recognising and accepting this is the first step to building bridges and opening the door for learning and understanding between us, doulas, and them, our end-of-life colleagues.

For those of us who work outside the tight and accepted framework of the industry we can often encounter resistance when engaging with the industry and indeed many other areas at the end of life. This resistance is perpetuated by fear and a lack of understanding. This is why community engagement and education is vital to what we are trying to achieve.

The key to successful engagement with end-of-life/death-care workers and professionals is in understanding where these people are coming from and working out a way to present our services as a viable and valuable addition to the services they already provide. To present our work in such a way that it is understood, that shows we are all on the same page and we all have the same goal of wanting to improve and enhance the grief and bereavement outcomes for the families we serve. This is the same for the funeral industry as it is the medical communities, nursing services, palliative and hospice organisations, carers, end-of-life social services, grief and bereavement counsellors, chaplains,

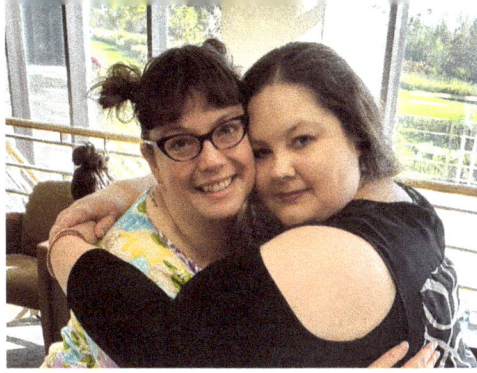

celebrants, complimentary therapists and the many other people who are considered stakeholders in this end-of-life space.

I got my introduction to the end-of-life space through a contemporary funeral home. I know intimately what kind of dedication it takes to do that work. I worked there for six years and for five and a half of those years it was owned by Australia's largest provider of funeral homes. In my years there I was the administration person, trouble shooter, record keeper, stock controller, information provider, and first point of call for families. I tracked market share and managed the accounts and invoices. I had the 'on call' phone for years before, after and during work and sometimes even while on holidays; I spent a long time as the only female funeral arranger. I worked as a pre-paid consultant and received a bunch of commission payments. I directed funerals, undertook community engagement and organised Christmas services.

By the time I was made redundant by the company I had worked in the mortuary doing body preparations, learned much about the cremation process and I was the acting location manager responsible for the staffing and asset allocation for day to day operations. I was available 24/7 no matter where I was, who I was with or what I was doing. This is a story more common than uncommon. This is work that is all consuming and often at the expense of family and friends.

It is from this perspective that we must approach those inside the end-of-life space – with the understanding that they are giving their all so that we are not attacking, minimising or belittling their efforts. Why would we position ourselves in opposition to such dedication? We are not saying that we do it better, instead we need to view our education of what we do as a value adding, a service of a different kind – similar in value and different in outcome. There is room in this world for people from various walks of life, various backgrounds and beliefs, various ethical and ethos spheres and the beauty of this is the wonderful and diverse choice that it delivers for the families.

Choice is not the enemy of market share, it is the framework within which people are able to make informed decisions, ones that are right for them and their families. If a business is offering what a family wants, no amount of choice will make them chose differently. If a family want to do things themselves, they should be supported to do so. Choice keeps businesses honest, prices competitive and the service offerings varied and transparent. Choice helps businesses learn what they can do, change and expand to offer in response to consumers wants and needs. At least that is the theory – the industries who work within end of life have been criticised for not delivering on these things in recent times – this has maybe hurt their market share more than any increase of choice ever could.

The reality is that people deserve choice: all the choices available to them. By our education we help the public to gain access to the length and breadth of what is truly possible.

The conversations that we need to be having with all the different people in the end-of-life space, on a very human one-on-one level, should not be about who does it better but about people; about families and agency and varied choices. It should be about different and diverse ways of honouring the dying and deaths – and ultimately the lives – of our fellow humans. It is about increasing public awareness, community capacity and the social capital that allows for the making of informed choices. There will always be people who choose the contemporary industry and that is a very valid choice if that is what is right for them. Some families would like a little of both, a blended service working with more than one business or group to achieve the end-of-life care and experience they want for themselves and their dead. It is important that we are able to work together when this is needed.

What those on the fringes seek to do through education and advocacy is carve the space for viable and valuable alternative services to exist alongside the conventional ones. Indeed, many of the services we are offering are a return to ways before the contemporary industry as we know it today was born. Gradually this change is coming, alternatives are now being taught in some USA mortuary schools and there are teachers who are open to the new way of doing things. This open approach will hopefully filter through the USA to Australia in the coming years.

People spending time with the dead during Dias de los Muertos,
the night of departure, Oaxaca, Mexico

THE VALUE OF STORYTELLING
AND LIVED EXPERIENCE

Stories are the missing and perhaps the forgotten, link between how things were and how we find them today. There is huge value in lived experience and storytelling: it is an important way to learn, share and grow. It is a way of learning that allows a person to weave in their own experiences and look through the lens of another. It provides rich perspectives and robust discussions without the textbook scientific facts and figures approach. Storytelling allows each person's experience to be valued and in an environment of shared learning, it builds capacity not only in the individual, but collectively in the community. Storytelling provides a platform for a shared narrative, the building of a framework of understanding around a topic where a person can develop their own interpretations into a solid foundation of understanding. This is especially important when considering end-of-life and death literacy.

Societies have been teaching their ways through storytelling for centuries. For many societies, stories contain the law, the ways of conduct, the rules about social interaction and the ways in which we approach the major life events, of which death is the final one.

The more people I speak to, the more I feel like it is stories, the stories of their lived experiences, that seems to matter at the end of life. With the world's current trend towards professionalisation and the need for statistics and facts and figures I think there's an overlooking of sorts; people's stories, their experiences, histories and the lessons they hold are somehow deemed anecdotal at best and are not given much weight in some circles. But we need to find a balance.

We as story holders at the end of life, need the academics. They provide invaluable work, especially when it comes to labelling, categorising and explaining things to governments and big business – and considering the need for funding and support in this space at present, this is imperative. However, we need to be reminded that it is not the only way to learn. Lived experience and the sharing of that is a necessary part of change, of building capacity and confidence. I believe that it is by tapping into those with lived experience, by encouraging people to tell their stories, that we are paving the way for others to start their own reclaiming of death.

Everyone I know who has come to the work in the end-of-life space has come through their own experience and story. Some may have inherited generational knowledge of caring for the dead, others have been brought to it through their own caring experiences and other have had it thrust upon them through the bad experiences they or others have had.

Regardless, in each of us there is a desire to do differently based on what has gone before us. It is a desire to serve and to enhance the grief and bereavement outcomes for ourselves and others. It is deeply personal and unquantifiable, which is why it so often gets labelled 'alternate'.

Sitting in the conferences throughout this Fellowship, talking to other researchers, professionals, trainers, academics and presenters as well as attendees, there is a common understanding that this work is experiential. It is deeply human and apart from storytelling, we in the West do not have a set quantifiable method of understanding the benefit and power of this work other than through lived experience and the telling of those experiences through story. Methods of qualitative research go some way to assist in honouring the value of storytelling but all too often the person is removed and within that removal we lose some often-important context.

Shared story telling within a community allows that community to write or re-write their narrative – to build their own way of interacting with death and understanding it. There is a support that comes with this as well. Stories draw us in. True stories, shared from that vulnerable place we all have, connect us to each other and create a bond of support, even between relative strangers. This is community capacity building at work and very little of it can be seen or measured other than how we choose to show up for each other.

One of the most interesting examples of storytelling and social narratives around death can be seen in the Dias de los Muertos celebrations. There is a very specific narrative around that time of the year, days for specific facets of the celebration, certain actions that take place at certain times. It is all heavily ritualised and while these rituals differ from place to place their story and meaning remain the same.

For the Mexicans, Dias de los Muertos is a sacred time and there are many narratives around why they do what they do. These are told through stories passed down through the generations, they often include stories of negative consequences visiting the families of ancestors who did not receive offerings, and there are similar cause and effect-style lessons. Importantly, these are not fairy tales, they are ancestral learnings.

The main narrative and understanding remain the same across all their pre-colonisation culture – this is a sacred time with the dead and within that there is a time for the preparation and arrival, a time to celebrate and remember them and a time for them to depart. This narrative permeates their entire lives, their grief and bereavement when a person dies and their connection to the elderly while they live. They look after each other and they know they will have set aside time to continue doing so in death.

Of all of the more than 50 interviews and conversations I have had through this Fellowship, everyone has had a story and in that story was a truth, a learning. People talk about death regardless of their skill, occupation or education, through the stories of their experiences. These are things that cannot be taught in doula trainings or mortuary schools. More weight needs to be attributed to our storytelling and we need to consider the stories we tell each other and those we leave for future generations. They will define how we do what we do.

I feel it is imperative that we document these stories and start to see them with a kind of reverence – not every story will fit everybody, but everyone can find a story that resonates with their own and within that is a special kind of growth and learning.

TRAINING AND THE ISSUES AROUND MICRO-CREDENTIALING

Perhaps one of the most pressing issues to arise from this Fellowship has been around the ideas of training, legitimacy building and the introduction of micro-credentialing. It is not unusual for professional services to have a peak body. Professions are accredited through that peak body and they provide support to those accredited by them. This can be seen in various industries. For a grassroots movement to offer this, however, is slightly problematic. My understanding is that for an entity to offer accreditation there must be responsibility, on some level, taken for its members and their actions. This is a level of liability unable to be afforded within newly formed bodies. So while in the USA they have organisations such as National Home Funeral Alliance and National End of Life Doula Association they are membership based for training, information, advocacy and community education but they have not been able yet to offer a national licence or other type of accreditation for their members.

How then, does an organisation build legitimacy with other stakeholders such as palliative care providers, hospices, nursing and care homes, medical institutions and many others where there is so little uniformity and so much diversity in the quality of training provided? Honestly, with a dozen different variations of titles and no clear definitions of the roles, this is a tall task. Enter micro-credentialing.

This is essentially proficiency based testing whereby at the successful conclusion of a set of questions and/or actions a proficiency mark is awarded to the practitioner and that then is a form of credential to show that a certain level of knowledge and expertise has been obtained. Similar to continuing professional development schemes in other industries, this proficiency is generally not for life and needs to be re-obtained each time the renewal falls due. This system then, does a few things and they can be summarised as follows:

- This means that the trainers need to gear their training towards the successful completion of the proficiency; people are less likely to pay for training if they are not equipped at the end of it to obtain the proficiency credentials.
- Micro-credentialing gives a kind of level playing field to practitioners, so that they all have achieved the same proficiency regardless of who they have trained with.

Taking time for tea and a spot of writing and research in Prague, Czech Republic

- The public (prospective clients), can have confidence in choosing a proficient practitioner because there is a standard that has been achieved.
- It builds confidence and legitimacy within medical and other institutions also providing professional end-of-life services.

However, there are points of great caution needed.

What is possible when we talk about micro-credentialing is creating just another role that people have to find money to pay for. Some of the best known and respected people in this space have expressed similar concerns. Additionally, by micro-credentialing we create the possibility of a kind of hierarchy where the people credentialed may feel entitled to charge more than those who are not, regardless of their experience and skill set – and in either case this will preclude anyone who cannot afford the service from having it.

Some people have taken radical approaches to ensure this is not the case. For example, Claire Turnham does not charge for her time but allows the families to choose what they pay her. Some people have argued that this work cannot be paid for and should be a service-based giving of time to the community. While some volunteer programs work well as a part of a much bigger picture (such as the CEOLP in Crestone Colorado), for the vast majority of solo practitioners this is not tenable and can be seen as a naïve idea. I am conscious of the very real fact, as Dr Annetta Mallon pointed out when we spoke at the NHFA Conference in Minnesota, that women (mostly) have done far too much unpaid labour in this world already.

Traditionally women have been the care givers at the end of life for countless generations. Now the roles are emerging for this work and women are realising that it is valued – in today's world people pay for the goods and services that are of value to them. So not unsurprisingly, women are now wanting to make a career out of this work.

I was reminded by Heather Massey and Zenith Virago – both, women who have been doing this and similar work at the end of life for decades and long before it had a name – that we as a movement run the risk of losing the true focus here. The focus is skilling families to care for their dead.

Home funerals are not about third parties stepping in and doing things for a family. Home funeral guides, practitioners and doulas are support roles that were designed to give guidance and support to the dying and their families at the end of life. Families are the ones in the best position to do this and we do not really want to create another paid-for service that takes the power away from families. We need to remember that families do not need a third party at all, unless they are needed for the fulfilment of some basic legal requirement.

How then do we reconcile these things? The conversation seems to circle back to micro-credentialing.

For doulas and other end-of-life practitioners, it is not unreasonable that payment be sought for their services, but how to make them not exclusionary? In order to be paid for end-of-life work as a doula the role needs to exist along with many other complimentary services at the end of life and for that there needs to be a certain amount of legitimacy, uniformity and confidence in the role and what is to be expected from it. Standardisation: micro-credentialing is the first step on the path to this.

When it comes to home funerals, Australia does not have the role of home funeral guide and doulas and practitioners are working in that space already, filling that role. This is not without its problems. In America, home funeral guides help a family navigate the after-death requirements; they are distinct from funeral directors because they are NOT hands-on with the body of the deceased and if they are invited to be hands-on by the family, they cannot take payment for that service. This is a clear line in the sand which most of the trainers I spoke to said they followed in their teachings. It has developed over the last few decades to be very clear and it is easily so, because USA requires strict licensing for funeral directing in most states.

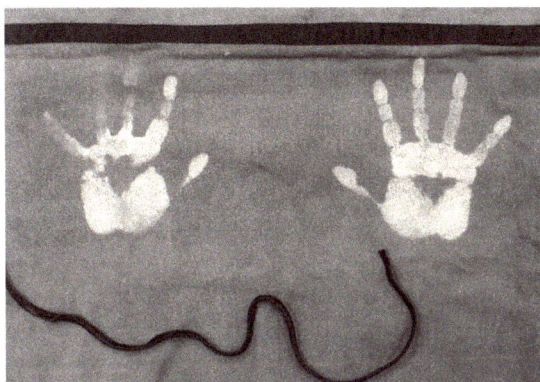

My handprints on 'The Little Black Dress', a burial garment made for MOMA (New York, USA), designed and created by Dr Pia Interlandi

In Australia, there is no licensing or formal qualification required to be a funeral director (only if you are going into business and opening a funeral home provider), so the line in the sand for doulas has not been so clear. As previously stated the role is largely undefined at present. What is slightly less known in Australia is the notion of being a 'prescribed business' or a 'regulated business'. That is, to be a business hands-on with the transport or care of human remains, you need to be approved as such by state authorities. While individual funeral directors are not licensed, each funeral home must be approved by the state.

In places where there is a clear separation between the role of a doula and the role of a funeral director, we are starting to see doulas work in conjunction with funeral directors; there is no crossover of function and therefore the role of doula is not a threat to the industry as it stands.

Australia is also on the brink of change. This year will see the introduction of a new Cert. IV in End of Life Doula and we are yet to see how this will impact the landscape. My instinct says the impact will be positive, that it will lay the most solid foundation we have so far as to the introduction of doula as an allied health professional. What that means on the ground in our hospitals and nursing homes, still remains to be seen.

It is also worth noting that as previously mentioned, no doula (or home funeral guide) that I spoke to in any country that I visited is making a full-time living out of the work that they are doing. In Australia as everywhere else, the only people making full-time incomes are those providing training and those approved or licensed to work as funeral directors in addition to their other role. This means that there is still a lot of work to do and a lot of education required and what we do not want is to create a range of people looking to supplement income by training in subjects they may or may not be sufficiently experienced in.

Before death, the doula remains a non-medical support to the dying and the family of the dying. After death, the doula remains a support to the family (only if the family want it), offering emotional, spiritual or planning support; the hands-on care of the deceased is not part of the role. That care, transport and anything else that is required is to be done by the family alone or by another regulated business they choose to engage. Importantly, the family can do everything themselves within the realms of the law.

This is the distinction being made around the world now and it is part of the defining being done to give clarity and confidence to those who are looking to include doulas in the legitimate end-of-life conversations. Without these clear lines of distinction in Australia it will be very difficult to gain traction and build the legitimacy we are starting to see take shape overseas.

The American NHPCO have created a Doula Council; as explained by Alua Arthur, part of this is because they have done the work to standardise the role and cement the confidence and expectations in it. Micro-credentialing is a big part of this confidence and legitimacy building. This could very well see doulas being included as paid positions in nursing and care homes and hospices nationwide.

I would welcome similar inclusive councils being founded in Australia.

Finally, not to be discounted is the very real possibility that if doulas held paid positions, it would also go a long way to address the problem of exclusion and equity. Some people just cannot afford to hire a private practitioner, but if it was a paid position just as in community nursing, or offered by any allied health provider, it could be accessed by those in need of it regardless of their financial circumstances.

In looking at the overall picture of alternative approaches and technologies, it would be remiss not to mention the many projects, platforms and organisations that exist and are well established where death disruption and capacity building intersect. I have not included them directly in this research; there are simply far too many. They are, however, a very valid part of this conversation as they are an integral component of how we as a society have arrived in the place we are today, more ready than ever for transparent conversations about death. It is from this place – the foundation that these provide – that we are able to look to the future.

The last decade has seen the start of a great many people instigating public conversations around dying and death using a variety of approaches. At their core, these approaches are designed to normalise end-of-life and death conversation; they are rooted in a firm belief that by entertaining these discussions a person can have far better end-of-life outcomes for themselves and the people around them.

Some of the best known platforms for end-of-life conversation and the building of death literacy within various communities are the models of Death Café and Death Over Dinner. Death Cafés have been held all over the world; they are meetings of people who come together without an agenda to talk about all kinds of death related topics and share their own experiences.

Death Over Dinner is a more structured event, where there is a host and set discussion points that the attendees receive prior to the dinner and the conversation is facilitated during the courses of the meal. Both of these movements, started by individuals, are now entities in their own right and have impacted the lives, and deaths, of thousands of people.

There are also other kinds of death focused groups that are emerging across the world, within local, national and international communities. Many of these groups have gained media traction and those that offer membership are seeing a regular increase in their numbers; they are all working at building community capacity and engaging with the wider public to educate, inform and advocate for the public's awareness and agency in the consideration of their own end of life.

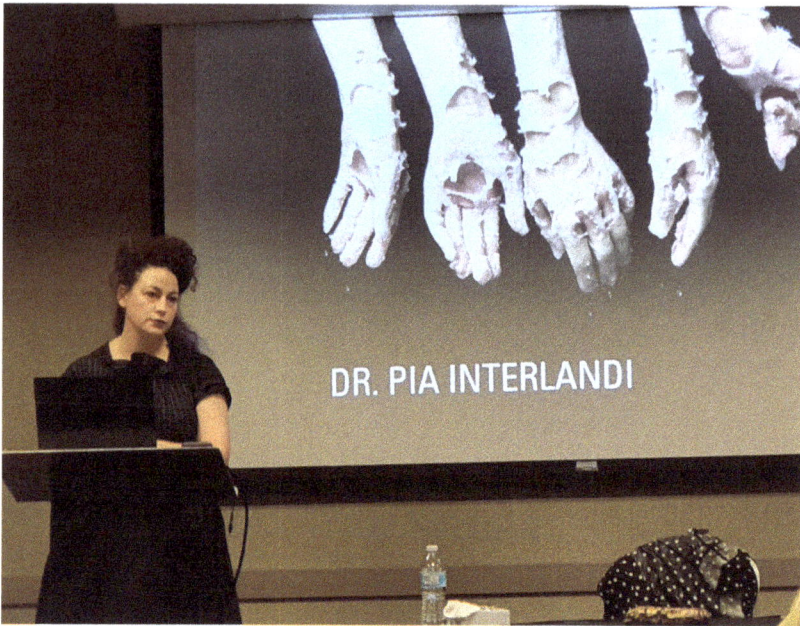

Dr Pia Interlandi lecturing about co-creating meaning through her work, Garments for the Grave at the 2019 National Home Funeral Alliance Conference, Minnesota, USA

The Order of the Good Death, the Collective for Radical Death Studies, Death Salon and the Australian Groundswell movement are among the many groups working to collectively push the agenda for a change in how we 'do' the end of life, and death. They are able to hold a presence on social media, host events and conferences, provide video and email content to the public and to initiate capacity building programs to further their goals and as such they pave the way for the many smaller groups doing similar things on a smaller scale.

Individuals such as Caitlin Doughty (Ask a Mortician), Alua Arthur, Dr Pia Interlandi, Melissa Unfred (The Modern Mortician), Carla Valentine (The Chick and the Dead), and Caleb Wilde (Confessions of a Funeral Director) have all built personal profiles which they are using as a platform to bring the various facets of their expertise in this space to a level of public awareness never seen before. They provide a personal and very human connection to what can sometimes be abstract ideas, by fearlessly telling their stories and sharing the stories of others.

These people are able to provide the public face for many end-of-life approaches. Whether they are funeral directors, doulas, designers, celebrants, lawyers, lecturers, morticians, embalmers or a combination of those roles, these people provide unique and personal perspectives through which the wider community can identify with, engage with and ultimately learn from – thus building community capacity on a large scale.

All of these platforms, people, groups and initiatives are providing new and innovative ways to bring end-of-life and death conversations to the general public. And this is the point. Regardless of the differences in these people, their background, approaches or training; regardless of the focus or intention of the platform, all of these ways and approaches exist because people have identified a need to increase death literacy and they believe in the extraordinary grief and bereavement outcomes that can be achieved when thought, consideration and honest conversation is had in relation to dying and death. That honesty will only be achieved when death becomes a normalised part of life and we have all of those listed here and many others to thank for their part in beginning to make it so.

APPENDIX B:
NOTES ON BURIAL AND CREMATION

As humans we have been commonly burying our dead in specific and communal places – cemeteries – for about five and a half thousand years, although there are some archaeological findings emerging suggesting it could be older than this.

From about the 7th century CE in Europe the burial of the dead was the domain of the church. Burial practices varied from place to place, from mass graves to walls, to vault and tomb interment. Ossuaries – places for the resting of mass amounts of bones after decomposition – were made, in some places due to space issues, and in others due to plague or similar contagions which subsequently required bodies to be buried in a short space of time.

Burials were organised and divided by social status nearly as early as burial is known to have begun. The wealthy were buried in the best places with the most elaborate markers or with many goods and possessions depending on the faith of the society at the time of burial.

Plagues and disease are not new but they have changed over time. The rapid population growth and subsequent overcrowding of the modern age (spurred on by the industrial revolution) saw the mass outbreak of disease and a steep rise in the death rate. People were buried in graveyards (defined then as a place of burial within church grounds) and the church was the centre of life – this meant that the living were continually among the death, with at times unhygienic burial practices and this perpetuated the cycle of disease.

Eventually, throughout Europe the burial in graveyards was legislated against and the dead were relegated to burial in cemeteries outside the city walls.

One of the first examples of this happening in Europe was in Paris – the Père-Lachaise Cemetery. This is one of the earliest examples of a European landscape-style cemetery that was not controlled by the church. It was the result of a law of 21 June 1804 that prohibited the burial in church graveyards, convents and cemeteries within the city walls.

Public health was also what drove these concerns in London and the UK and in 1819 the first cemetery was opened in Norwich for people of all beliefs. The first 50 years of the 1800s in London saw the population more than double and

A monumental grave, designed to tell the story of grief and loss around the death, Prague, Czech Republic

all of the church graveyards become very overcrowded. This, combined with the churches' being the centre of town activity, compromised systems like the water supply and resulted in epidemics of diseases like cholera – which killed 52,000 people there in 1831. Legislation followed and eventually the dead were buried outside city walls.

According to the Australian Museum[9], the earliest known method of cremation was a log pyre, with pitch and gum sometimes added to the firewood. There is evidence of cremation dating back 40,000 years. Australian Indigenous cremation is still referred to in Tasmanian State Legislation and takes place as an open-air pyre-style cremation.

The practice of open-air cremation was introduced to the western world by the Greeks around 1000 BCE. This was a response to dealing with the casualties of war. Corpses were cremated on the battlefield and the ashes were gathered up and sent to the homeland for ceremony and interment. The Romans followed the Greeks in cremating their military heroes. Cremation became a status symbol.

It was a process connected to pagan traditions and as such the early church was not in support of this method of body disposal. After ~400 CE, cremation was only used in some places in emergencies, such as outbreaks of the Black Death. In the Eastern traditions, cremation has continued for centuries. In places like Varanasi in India it is considered the holy way to deal with human remains.

According to an article by Thomas Lacquer[10], cremation of the dead was normal in the 1st century AD and by the 4th century it was the exception. By the 9th century cremation is seen as pagan and the ruler Charlemagne insisted that the Germanic tribes under his rule abandon their pyres and associated pagan practices. By the 11th century it was widely accepted that the only proper place for a dead body was in a church graveyard, so much so that exclusion from burial on holy 'sacred' ground was considered detrimental to one's soul. Only heretics, those who had died by suicide, the ex-communicated and witches were burned – alive – and their ashes scattered.

In 1794 the world had been burying people for thousands of years – excluding the heretics. In France the Jacobite revolutionaries reintroduced cremation for the common man as an explicitly public alternative to church-based burial. The Jacobites were responsible for the first full-scale Roman style public cremation in almost 2000 years and the first of its kind in France for over 1000 years.

The first body to be cremated was that of a doctor, Charles Nicholas Beauvais de Préau, a member of the national assembly from the department of the Seine, who had been imprisoned after a royal takeover of the city of Toulon. When the city was re-taken by Napoleon he was moved to Montpellier, being too sick to travel back to Paris. He died 28 March 1794. The next day the revolutionary government reinstated cremation and announced to the public that *the 'martyr of liberty would be cremated in a civil ceremony'*[11]. This had the effect of keeping his body out of the hands of the Church and a year later, on 11 November 1795, cremation in France was made legal.

The revival of cremation in the UK did not come until the 1870s when the surgeon to Queen Victoria published a book on cremation called 'Cremation: The Treatment of the Body After Death'. He formed the Cremation Society of England and cremation was finally legislated as a legal process in 1884.

The first crematorium was built in America in 1876 in Washington Pennsylvania and five years later the New York Cremation Society was formed.

Wall crypts, above-ground crypt and free-standing crypt on the Isola di San Michele, Venice, Italy

In Italy, cremation had many challenges. It was the Freemasons comprising doctors, scientists, progressives, positivists – they were republicans and supporters of things anti-clerical – who advocated for cremation. The first legal cremation was given the green light on 22 January 1876 by a government official and the Freemasons: the first person to be cremated was a businessman and Freemason.

The Church saw cremation as an affront to them, they forbade membership to cremation societies, and the act of joining was seen as hostile to the Church. But cremations continued to spread, through Europe including Germany and Russia despite debates over socialist and communist approaches. The Pope lifted the ban on cremations on 5 July 1963 and in 1966 it became permissible for priests to conduct a cremation service.

The Australian Museum records that Australia's first crematorium was built at Rookwood in NSW in 1925[12]. It is now the oldest continually operating crematorium in Australia.

The point to this history is in the context of how we value our current body disposal methods and traditions and how willing we may be to rethink them. We as a society need to remember that in Australia, we have inherited our modern current burial and cremation practices from Europe (despite the allowance for Aboriginal cremation in places which is a right that exists under specific circumstances only). These more contemporary practices of burial and cremation as we know them today were entrenched in European social convention long before the colonisation of Australia and they have changed, been adopted, outlawed and reinstated through the years in response to plagues, epidemics, disasters and population explosions; all the things which as a more modern society, we have not experienced in our post-colonial history. These methods of body disposal are from a much longer chequered history of humanity and we have never stopped to question them or sought to alter or expand on them.

We have never questioned how well they serve us here in Australia.

Over the centuries we have only become further detached from our dead and now as a society we find, along with much of the western world that we have no agency over our dead. And yet, they are still our people.

En Via participant and host of our group in San Miguel de Ville with Viviana Ruiz Boijseauneau, the then Managing Director of Fundación En Vía, Oaxaca, Mexico

APPENDIX C:
NOTES ON EN VIA AND ETHICAL TOURISM

In Oaxaca I toured with a micro-financing not-for-profit group called En Via. I wanted to be able to meet locals and see the true Dias de los Muertos without being a 'tourist' and ignorantly participating in the cultural appropriation, which is a much talked about and abhorrent practice. I decided one of the best ways would be to take small group tours with a not-for-profit organisation working to build capacity within communities and supporting their financial growth. It was a nice way to give back.

En Via started in 2008 and by 2010 it was not-for-profit; they have a staff of six full-time people, 30 volunteers and they fund loans for over 250 women across six rural villages. Years ago, there was a bank in Mexico which started as not-for-profit and was able to help local people, but when it became for-profit the many self-employed people found access to funds hard. The average interest rate in Mexico is 76 percent for loans making them largely unaffordable.

The En Via model is simple and designed to teach people how to build a successful business. In Mexico the notion of success is quite different from that in the western world. Where poverty is normal in many places in Mexico, success is simply having enough to maintain the life sustaining basics for a family without struggle. Often the women who are a part of the En Via program greatly exceed this in terms of success.

En Via only lend money to women – they are known to repay loans more consistently and also spend more time and effort investing in families than the men do – but they have also been largely undervalued and this is part of their growing independence. Socially, they were in very much the same position as the majority of the rest of the world: second to men; equality has reached here only in a limited capacity and only in the more recent times.

The En Via model goes like this: women get on a waiting list. They do an 8-class course which is about sustainable business practices, before they get access to any money. They learn about using the profits to grow business, marketing, taking control of stock and purchasing materials. This is important because many of the villages have been largely patriarchal, and this education is new to them. This process is changing women's lives. The women we met said that while they had to leave school early to work in the family business, their children are able to stay in school longer and have a better and longer education due to the income the women are now earning.

In some cases, the wider community benefits from this program through building businesses to a point where they can employ other people from their own and neighbouring villages. For the first time, these women are also in a position to save money. En Via holds the courses in the communities and travels to the communities to both lend and collect the money and repayments.

The women are lent their funds in groups of three and they are each responsible for finding the women who will make up their team of three. They each receive 1500 pesos (AU$101.00) and they have 10–15 weeks to repay the funds. Using the model of only lending to three and group accountability, they have a 99 percent repayment rate. They will only accept the group repayment in full and if a woman has a bad week, she is able to leave a down payment of no less than 20 pesos (AU$1.35) and repay the balance in addition to the following week's repayment. If no repayment is made for a week each woman is fined 60 pesos (AU$4.05).

From top: The complex where En Via's office is and where the tours leave from, Oaxaca, Mexico; Flores de Muertos, the flower that families search for and gather to place on their altars during Dias de los Muertos

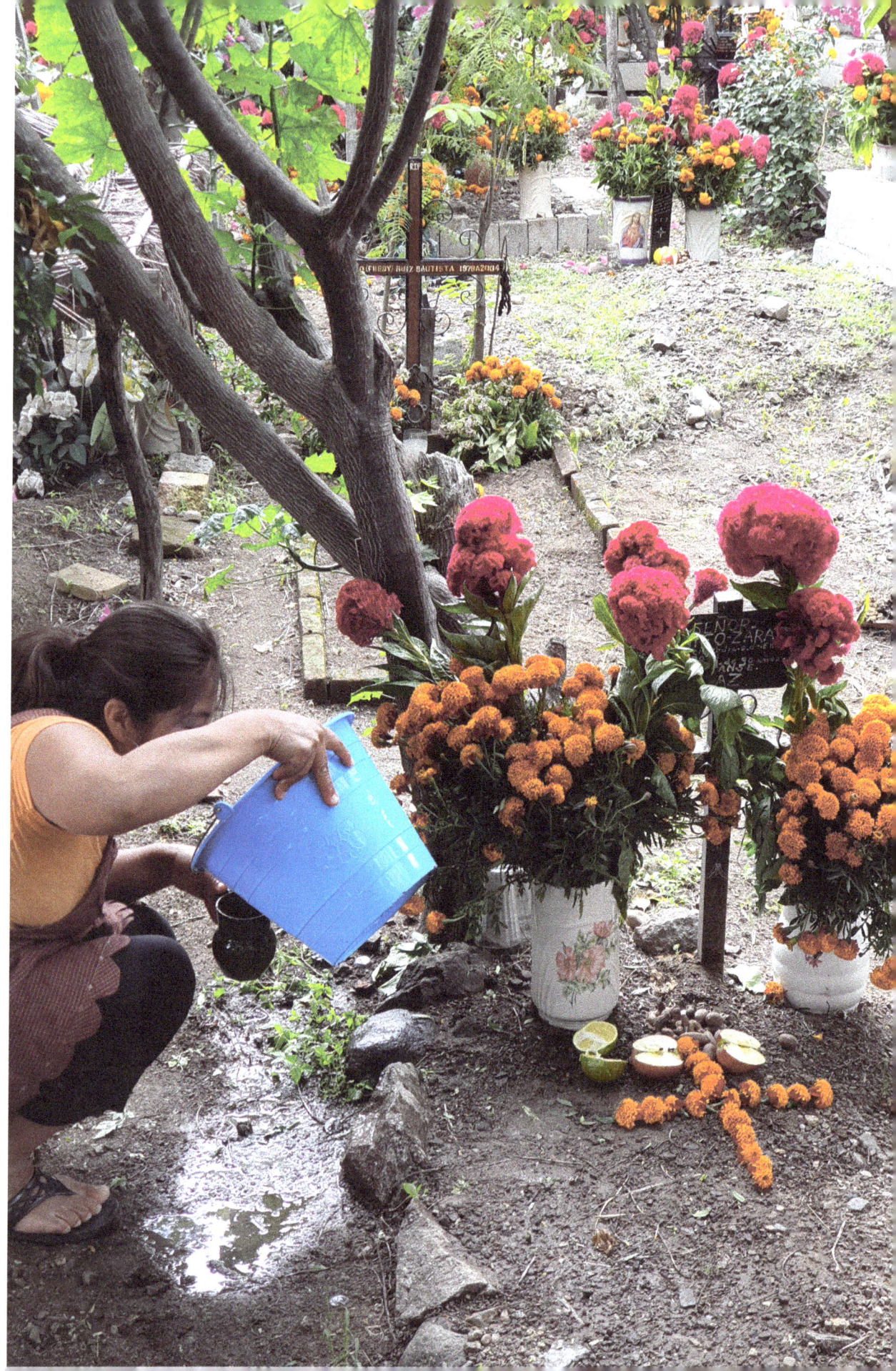

En Via does not vet the recipients, they believe that women will only go into business with other women they trust and usually they are family groups. The women can change in and out of groups over time as well. Once the loan is repaid in full, they are able to borrow again in increasing amounts. They increase by 1000 pesos (AU$67.60) every time. En Via also hold weekly meetings in the communities for the business partner groups and for women to come and find out about the program. They sign up on a wait list if they are interested.

En Via will fund any kind of business. They have a beauty salon, people who make chocolate, weavers, those who raise chickens etc. At the end of the successful repayment of a loan the women are generally required to accept a tour group such as the kind of experience I went on with them. During the Dias de los Muertos, however, it is voluntary since this is such a personal and sacred family time. The funds from these tours allow them to lend the money to the women interest-free, continue the program and offer free English classes within communities. They do not get funding from the government.

This is the context with which to understand the interviews I did and the learning I undertook about Dias de los Muertos. I visited two different communities over three days, and I spoke with various locals of different ages, genders and backgrounds. These people took me into their homes, shared their stories and showed me the graves of their ancestors. I have collated this information for the most part rather than recorded separate interviews. I was able to speak to people through translators and in the family homes of local Zapotec people. In Mexico City, I hired an English-speaking guide.

Left: Grave cleaning in the village Teotitlan del Valle, Mexico

APPENDIX D:
NOTES ON IMPORTANT END OF LIFE RESEARCH

Many articles, reports and much research has been done in recent times in Australia and abroad, looking at how we do the end of life and why it is the way it is. This has framed our understanding and goes some way to explain our current approaches to dying and death.

What follows are my notes, made from reading the work that has been done. They are not meant as an academic summary, simply my own understanding and summation of some of the publicly available publications, findings and articles, which I found to provide relevant contributions to the Australian context of this conversation.

Memorial to John Lennon in Central Park, New York City, USA

How Dying Works, Molly Edmonds (USA)

- How we see death has changed over the years. There has been the idea of brain death, the 'Balfour's Test' which was sticking needles into bodies to look for reactions.
- Dying of old age is a relatively new thing; longevity has meant that there has been an increase in degenerative diseases. Organ harvesting is a possibility now and so we have had to determine what is death while a body's cells have not died.
- Biological death begins 4–6 minutes after clinical death... 'different cells die at different speeds, so the length of the dying process depends on which cells are deprived of oxygen'. This is why some organs can be harvested after 'death' (when the body is no longer breathing) and others cannot.
- A body starts to cool soon after death and the body temperature drops about 0.83 degrees Celsius every hour until it reaches room temperature.

What does a public health perspective bring to understandings of ageing and the end of life? Merryn Gott and Christine Ingleton, 01.12.2011 (NZ)

- Bruce Rumbold argues 'health promoting palliative care' approach can improve existing services for aged/dying and identify wider social reforms to develop age friendly communities.
- Need to consider the effects of bereavement on health and wellbeing if the public health approach is going to be fully responsible to individual and community needs.
- Death and dying are hardly mentioned in old textbooks and writing on ageing.
- Palliative care is largely a response to 'out of time' deaths from cancer.
- Specialist palliative care focused on the core business of hospice – cancer care.
- Only recently are policy makers becoming more aware that community engagement is needed.
- Dying is a matter for community management – health services should respond to it, not direct it.
- Palliative care relatively rarely talks about a good death as a health outcome.
- Dominance of clinical priorities in treating life-threatening illness encourages people to be passive recipients of technical care rather than active agents in their own lives.

- Capacity to have agency in your health – patients to work with health professionals, not submit to them, people might then keep agency in their decision making around EOL.
- Health promoting approach pays attention to settings in which old people die and the needs of late life and how communities and services respond and meet them.
- Health promotion in aged care does not talk about death (should do, this would provide empowerment).
- Argument for home care – 'occupying particular familiar spaces or places can support a sense of competence and help mediate other unavoidable changes'.
- Changing nature of social relationships incorporates the living and the dead.
- Diminishment, decline and decay. Dying still kept private and resisted. Attitude they need to be endured with medical support. Mindset changes needed. Change attitude – not to prolong life but to prolong independence.
- Death treated as a medical event – transform this to social – stop dying being seen as the antithesis of living.
- 'The medicalisation of old age – which is a social strategy administered rather than determined, by health systems – appears a major barrier to achieving healthy dying in old age'.
- If dying is a social event then people's citizenship shapes discussions not their patient status, palliative care can then develop a health service to respond to EOL as a community concern.
- Need to encourage autonomy and agency in policies.

Bringing our Dying Home, Assoc Prof. Debbie Horsfall, Kerrie Noonan and Assoc Prof. Rosemary Leonard, May 2012 (AUS)

- What if we had a national conversation about EOL?
- What if the Home Death Movement named itself as such and claimed its place at the decision-making table?
- Carers and those in the outer circle have a primary motivation to keep life as normal as possible for the primary carer and immediate family.
- People and community's death literacy develops as a result of being caring of dying.

- About 2.3 million people in Australia provide long term care to loved ones (Palliative Care 2004) – unpaid carers contribute $20 billion to economy.
- 'Good Death' has been replaced with 'managed death' requiring medical support.
- Growing acknowledgment about the lack of grassroots approaches to EOL care.
- Concerns about sustainability of current care models.
- Community approaches allow for community members to take steps and make new and constructive ways to increase their own capacity for EOL care.
- Mentoring in EOL enriches capacity of the dying and their families.
- Networks – friends of carers, friends of the dying person, friends of the family, work colleagues, neighbours, community organisations, spiritual groups, service clubs, shopkeepers, animals – people expressed desire to keep connected.
- Phone calls and communication built into the dying person's care plan.
- Agency – dying person may very well want input and take control re connections socially.
- Digital communication was useful to connect carer and the whole care network.
- Some people fear the judgement of asking for help so remain determined to 'cope'.
- Striving for normality in extraordinary circumstances.
- 'Transformations occurred in people's skills and knowledge about death and dying; about the tasks of caring for people and about being a good friend. Attitudes to death, in particular dying at home, were changed. In fact, a great deal of experimental learning took place at an embodied and emotional level' – this is developing death literacy due to participation in caring for the dying.
- Experiences increase death literacy and community benefit as people share their experiences through story telling.
- 'An experience is just that, unless reflection on that experience takes place, transforming it into learning and possibilities for future actions'.
- Transformative experiences – people reflect deeply on previous deaths and their own. This personal development ripples out in material ways into the wider community.

- Empowerment and social structures needed for community to increase capacity to care.
- Many supportive social structures around death were lost due to the medicalisation of death.
- Dying at home takes a community.
- Unpaid caring work in the home can be as barrier to community participation and can be a cause for social isolation.
- Caring does not need to drain social capital or be isolating. Can actually contribute to social capital by growing the network of relationships.

End of Life at Home. Co-Creating an Ecology of Care
Assoc Prof. Debbie Horsfall, Dr Ainslie Yardley, Prof. Rosemary Leonard, Kerrie Noonan and Dr John Rosenburg, May 2015 (AUS)

- Australian policy of health promoting palliative care is not sustainably translating to practice.
- Existing relationships and networks affect the ability to care. Everyone is changed through the process of giving care.
- Care givers can provide in-home care with no prior knowledge or experience.
- Caring network maximises the wellbeing benefits of caring.
- An effective network –
  - One or more people with the experience of death
  - Can be any size, average is 16
  - Comprises family, friends, neighbours, colleagues
  - Service providers are essential but part of the outer network along with schools, churches, clubs, community groups and businesses
  - Can be initiated or spontaneous
  - Most likely exist when a person who is part of a community is dying.
- Participating in home death raises death literacy.
- Relationships between carers and formal service providers can be weakened by the insensitivity of service providers or by poor or inappropriate service provision.
- Formal service providers are appreciated when they go over and above.
- Need to maintain strong identity and sense of belonging.
- More need for health promoting palliative care policies.
- Palliative Care 2011 Australia – of approximately 140,000 Australians who die each year, 80 percent want to die at home and 16–20 percent do die at home.

- Rumbold 2010 – average length of community based palliative care is 119 days of which 117 are provided by families and friends etc. People do most of the dying at home, but they do not die there. They die in a place not of their choosing.
- Death was a social and community event, now it has been medicalised.
- HPPC has been adopted by government and Palliative Care Australia however there is a lack of commitment to the community component.
- Caring is seen as an intimate act and a personal expression of love.
- Carers co-ordinate their services but not always their networks or the community responses.
- People have capacity to do things when they are caring for another, things that they never dreamed of doing.
- Struggles were financial, geographical around service provision, lack of access to information, employment needs.
- Some of the greatest struggles were with hospitals, GPs and other formal medical services.
- Lack of community capacity – emotional maturity and resilience, inexperience, lack of cohesion and social isolation.
- Carers found it harder when there was no community support.
- Sense of injustice – the dying person contributed for decades to society but there is little/no financial support at the end of their lives.
- Some hospitals/facilities fail to acknowledge the end of life.
- Formal service providers include – GPs, palliative care teams, community nurses, pharmacists, home care services, massage and other therapy services.
- Clinical care and equipment a benefit of formal service providers – also access to other services families were otherwise unaware of.
- Being known to service providers helps navigate the system and increases flexibility and quality of the services provided.
- Some service providers can be obstructive; this can result in bad or lack of services and can impact psychologically. This can also discredit the carer's role.
- The 'professionalism' of formal service providers was seen in contract to the informal provision of support by carers and network members. On some occasions, this divide meant the withdrawal of formal support if patients did not comply with the directive to be admitted to hospital'.

- 'Death literacy then is the outcome of people's experiences of, and learning about, death and dying. Once this happens, death literacy becomes a resource that people and communities can use, thus strengthening their capacity for future caring'.
- Carers and networks said that they learned how to live more deeply and fully; to appreciate the moments; not to worry if the washing was done or not; tolerance for themselves and others; that they are capable of showing up and doing what was needed.
- The process of caring at home changes attitudes – makes people want to give back.
- Importance placed on creating a caring space – nonclinical – focus on how the dying person experiences the space as well as the network (including respite spaces and creative spaces).
- 'Carers wanted people with expertise around – the voice of authority to validate what they were doing. They might not have wanted someone telling them what to do, but they did want technical advice: This is how to inject, medicate, turn, bath, cope with seizures etc.'
- 'There was no equivocation about what dying "well" meant. It is not necessarily being pain free, completely at peace, without fear, anxiety or regret – for the dying person or the carer – but at home, with a sense of purpose in a collective human task, surrounded by love and the known so that dying people retain their identities by staying connected to the people and places that are meaningful for them.'
- 'Social change – this is needed so that communities can accept that they do have an important role at the end of life, a role that will ultimately strengthen both the community's capacity to care and the social capital available to them to invest in other developments'.

Developing Death Literacy, Kerrie Noonan, Debbie Horsfall, Rosemary Leonard, John Rosenburg; January 2016 (AUS)

- 'Death Literacy is designed as a set of knowledge and skills that make it possible to gain access to understand and act upon end-of-life and death care options'.
- Community development builds the ability and capacity to increase knowledge about the end of life, it allows communities to look after each other.

- There are people and communities that have a high level of death literacy with context specific knowledge about their death system – different communities have different 'death systems' or ways of doing death.
- Death Literacy is a form of 'practical wisdom'. Greater levels of death literacy give people the capacity to care for each other at the end of life.
- 'The act of end-of-life care-giving provides a deeply personal connection to death and dying'.
- 'Caring at home, where carers are able to be hands-on with the dying person and the dead body, that provides and embodies learning experience, invites reflection and meaning making'.
- People gain a network and a greater appreciation of friends and family. People see dying as a part of life.
- Death literacy does not just happen inside the context of the traditional modes of health education – it is community knowledge.
- Caring for a dying person is an opportunity for community development.

Beyond Taboos, 2017 (AUS)

Statistics from research undertaken in Australia by Groundswell, in conjunction with Western Sydney University and the Wicking Trust

- 29 percent of people have contributed to the 'hands-on' care of a person dying.
- 18 percent have given medications to a person dying.
- 45 percent can offer support to people with a dying family member but only 28 percent feel able to advocate for a dying person about medical intervention.
- 19 percent can care for a body after death.
- 51 percent of people have a Will.
- 43 percent of people have experienced the death of someone close to them under the age of 16.
- 20 percent of people know how to navigate the health system to support a dying person to receive care.
- 33 percent know how to navigate the funeral industry.
- 19 percent knew how to navigate the aged care system to advocate for a person's end-of-life wishes.
- 63 percent have sat with someone who was dying.
- 44 percent have sat with a person after death.

- 40 percent regularly participate in rituals to remember someone who has died.
- 39 percent have witnessed the death of a person.
- 20 percent keep ashes or care for a grave.
- 14 percent have helped care for a dead body.
- 9 percent of people know what an end-of-life doula does.
- Less than 20 percent know about the laws regarding body disposal, funeral requirements, dying at home, carer and bereavement leave.
- 29 percent cared hands-on for the dying – less than half of that, 14 percent, cared for the dead.
- 39 percent witnessed a death and only 14 percent cared for them.
- 44 percent spent time after death with a body but only 14 percent gave care.

It's Your Funeral, Prof. Sandra van der Laan, University of Sydney; 2017 (AUS)
- During the 20th century Australian death-care shifted from family to institutions.
- Prior to WW1 women tended death beds, prepared body and looked after it until funeral.
- In just 30 years after culture shifted, 'death denial' began and grief privatised.
- Consumer choice is dependent upon the consumer knowing the options that exist.
- Funeral Homes professional fee includes labour, which has been estimated at 24-40 hours per funeral. Overall labour and purchases account for 66 percent of total revenue while profit is 12 percent of revenue (Figure 24-40 hours comes from PSA(1992) where AFDA estimates 35-40 hours).

Palliative Care – The New Essentials, Julian Abel, Allan Kelleher, Aliki Karapliagou; Published 09.03.2018 (UK)
- 'The Social Justice basis for this approach [public health model of palliative care] responds to the crucial need for equity of care irrespective of age, background, diagnosis or cause of death'.
- The outcome of uniting professional care with community resource is inclusive care for the recipients.
- The World Health Organization defines palliative care as 'an approach

that improves the quality of life of patients and their families facing the problems associated with life-threatening illness, through prevention and relief of suffering by means of early identification and impeccable assessment and treatment of pain and other problems, physical, psychosocial and spiritual'.

- Difference between specialist and generalist palliative care – specialist palliative care is needed when patients require a complex assessment and specialist therapeutic knowledge. Generalist palliative care is routine care combined with social support and care.
- Non-cancer patients are underrepresented although they have comparable needs.
- UK figures – non-cancer patients are only about 11 percent of palliative patients. They are falling through the gaps.
- Networks of care – inner and outer circles of care. 3 of 10 people closely related to the person with illness. Outer circle 5–20 people – average is 16. These people help with 'stuff' like shopping and are not necessarily close to the person with the illness.
- Social prescribing – a way of connecting and reconnecting people to their communities.
- 'Professional support is incomplete without community support, especially in matters to do with quality and continuity of care'.
- Civic program, compassionate communities, generalist palliative care and specialist palliative care. All need to work together.
- 'Civic engagement in end-of-life care is not fully understood yet in societies where health care is perceived as a professional responsibility'.
- Cancer patients are more likely to die at home than non-cancer patients due to the lack of palliative care in community for the non-cancer patients.
- People who are encouraged to engage with the end of life and its care form beneficial partnerships with health care professionals and services and are able to assist in end-of-life care.
- 'Meaning and value in care is equally obtained in the context of supportive communities, and the same principal applies to physical care'.
- Emergency admissions to hospital that do not recognise end-of-life care undermines the opportunity to build resilient networks and prepare for care at home.

- 'Adverse circumstances at time of death complicate bereavement experiences and lead to longer-term poor health outcomes'.
- When community resources have been built there can be support groups and short term support networks that can be used around the health care resources and support.
- Long term resilient networks are best started early in an illness.
- 'Compassionate Communities rely upon the principal of civic responsibilities to care for end-of-life needs, and their formation can be initiated by healthcare services or community and charitable organisations alike'.
- It is estimated that bereavement impacts hospital inpatient days – adds to the cost of healthcare between 16.2 million pounds UK and 23.3 million.
- Experience of caring is not limited to the carer but extends through the whole caring network.

What Role do Death Doulas Play in End-Of-Life Care?
Deb Rawlings, Jennifer Tieman, Lauren Miller-Lewis, Kate Swetenham; Published 29.08.2018 (AUS)

- Refers to End of Life Doula Role as similar to that of an 'eldest daughter' or palliative care nurse.
- We do not understand the role of the doula properly yet.
- Other names – death midwifes, psychopomp (a guide of souls), stervensbergeleding (Dutch for 'dying guide'), lay navigator (used in oncology), death sitter and amicus mortis.
- Hard to pinpoint where the drive has come from for the role of the doula in this place.
- Some death doulas do work under the auspices of formal palliative care services or are seen to augment palliative care or hospice services – in these models death doulas are voluntary, providing non-medical care.
- Historically the family care-giving responsibilities fall on women. Eldest daughters in unpaid work. It is a disproportionate expectation.
- If doulas are acting as pseudo-professional (recording progress, patient info, staying informed, anticipating medical issues) they risk overlapping and replacing palliative care nurses.
- High costs as end-of-life makes fee-for-service doula work not viable.
- Need to engage media to understand the role of death doulas.

- Need to acknowledge that patient, carer and family views and experiences about death doulas have not been heard yet.

Final Report – *Compassionate Communities Feasibility Study* By NOUS; 06.07.2018 (AUS)

- An increase of people dying at home and consequent reductions in use of beds in institutions will require broad reforms across community, government, health services, systems – need to embed the public health approaches into palliative care.
- 1986 Ottawa Charter (Released by World Health Organization) framework for the growth of public health. States a shared responsibility for the promotion of health. Public health approaches to the end of life grew from this.
- In the late 1990s Professor Allan Kellehear developed the 'health promoting palliative care approach' looking at early intervention and social approaches to dying.
- Compassionate Communities are a part of this public health approach. Developed by Kellehear: describes community networks playing a role in caring at the end of life. It goes hand in hand with specialist palliative care and generalist palliative care reforms.
- 2005 Kellehear developed the Compassionate Cities Charter. It is a list of 13 social changes a city can adopt to become a Compassionate City.
- According to ABS (2013) the number and proportion of older Australians is expected to continue to grow – by 2056 it is projected that there will be 8.7 million older Australians, approx. 22 percent of the population. This means more people living with life limiting, life threatening and terminal illness.
- Australian expenditure on health in real time has grown an average of 5.3 percent per year. GDP has only grown 3.1 percent per year, this is largely unsustainable.
- Social care needs at the end of life are not sufficiently met.
- People at the end of life often experience social isolation and stress.
- Need to de-professionalise and de-medicalise the dying process
- HELP framework (Healthy End of Life Program) – one common framework to describe compassionate communities
- Common types of activities used in Compassionate Communities – care and support, community development, community partnerships, awareness raising, community activation, advocacy and policy

- Improved quality of life and wellbeing and personal growth and learning, greater self identity and sense of belonging for people at EOL who experience the Compassionate Communities model
  - Also for the families – increased death literacy, reduced stress and anxiety, reduced burden of care on informal care givers
  - Also for communities – growth of social capital and capacity building, growth of formal and informal partnerships and improved access to resources
  - Also for health professionals – reduced burden on health and social care, reduced likelihood of compassion fatigue
  - Also for the broader sector – reduced palliative related length of hospital stays
- Reduced cost of care per patient
- National bereavement survey data indicates that the majority of bereaved people rely on families and friends for their support and have had the best outcomes doing this (as opposed to people who have relied on health professionals for the same thing).
- Proposes implementation plan for Compassionate Communities in Australia (p29)
  - Integrate community provision of palliative care and end-of-life care into public health.
  - Draw on community strengths to create a supportive environment.
  - Strengthen community development and action.
  - Develop individual knowledge and skills about the end of life.
  - Re-orient health services to work in partnership with community.
- Individuals can still experience stigma around asking for help which can result in prevention of receiving care needed.

My Notes:

From the literature referred to above, the following key things can be considered as imperative to this conversation and the context from which I approached this research:

- We are missing out on the empowerment that is shown to come with being involved in end-of-life care.
- There is a real need to increase community involvement at the end of life.

Offrenda in the Novembre 20 Market, dedicated to the stall holders who have died in Oaxaca, Mexico

- Current end-of-life approaches are not delivering the outcomes in dying, death, grief or bereavement that society says they want.
- There is a sharp increase in the projected numbers of people dying in the next 35 years.
- Our current trajectory of care is considered financially unsustainable.
- There is a growing number of medical professionals lending their support to the call for a change in the approach to the end of life and the importance of the roles that community and other non-medical supports play in this space.
- After-death care is only considered in a limited capacity and remains largely unexplored.
- There is increasing academic interest and engagement in this space but there is a lack of government and health commitment to the development and implementation of the policies, processes and other structures required to make a positive difference.
- The space held by end-of-life doulas is relatively new and still being defined.

GLOSSARY OF ABBREVIATIONS AND TERMS

Family-led funeral – A ceremony that is organised by the family/friends/community of the deceased and held in any location of their choosing

Home death care – The care of a deceased person's body in the home of the family or that person's place of residence as provided by the family/friends/community of that person

Death literacy – The level of knowledge and awareness of end-of-life options, processes, systems and choices available

End of life doula – A person who provides non-medical support and guidance to a dying person and/or their family

Home funeral guide – An American term for a person who gives guidance in regard to the paperwork and legal requirements as well as logistical advice to a family providing hands-on body care and ceremony to their dead

Natural burial – The process of burial in a shallow depth grave using chemical-free preparations, no coffin or an eco-friendly one, natural protein-based fibre done in a way to enhance decomposition

Alkaline hydrolysis (AH) – A process of reduction of human tissue whereby the elements of the body return to a liquid state and are placed back into the water cycle

Community capacity – The ability, skills and knowledge within a group of people to successfully complete a set of actions and tasks with confidence, lend support to each other while doing so and pass those skills onto others

Compassionate communities – A model of community care whereby community members are trained and engaged to look after each other through a well-developed network of communication channels and services

Hospice – Hospice refers to both a type of care and a place of care for people nearing the end of life.

Palliative care – A system of care and support that focuses on living well with a terminal or life limiting diagnosis. Palliative care also relates to the final stages of end-of-life care.

Contemporary funeral industry – This term refers to the standard funeral industry as it exists in contemporary society.

NHFA – National Home Funeral Alliance USA

NEDA – National End of Life Doula Alliance USA

NHPCO – National Hospice and Palliative Care Organisation USA

NDAN – Natural Death Advocacy Network AUS

CEOLP – Crestone End of Life Project

Disruptive technologies – A disruptive technology is a new development or approach which causes disruption to an already established system of conduct or thinking.

A public memorial placed in Hollywood, showing a public display of mourning and grief, Hollywood Boulevard, Los Angeles, USA

SOURCES

- Abel J, Kellehear A, Karapliagou A. Palliative care – the new essentials. Ann Palliat Med. 2018 Apr;7(Suppl 2):S3-S14. doi: 10.21037/apm.2018.03.04. PMID: 29764169

- Australian Institute of Health and Welfare 17 July 2019, 'Deaths in Australia' Web Report https://www.aihw.gov.au/reports/life-expectancy-death/deaths-in-australia/contents/summary

- Australian Institute of Health and Welfare, 22 May 2019, 'Palliative Care Services in Australia', Web Report https://www.aihw.gov.au/reports/palliative-care-services-in-australia/palliative-care-services-in-australia/contents/palliative-care-in-residential-aged-care

- Australian Museum, 'Stages of Decomposition' ©The Australian Museum 2019 [Name of main publication]

- Costandi, Mo, 'Life After Death: The Science of Human Decomposition', The Guardian 5 May 2015

- Duffy, Andrew. 'More Research Needed', Ottawa Citizen, 25 July 2019, Ontario Canada https://ottawacitizen.com/news/local-news/more-research-needed-on-low-temperature-liquid-cremation-public-health-ontario-says

- Edmonds, Molly "How Dying Works" 12 January 2009 https://health.howstuffworks.com/diseases-conditions/death-dying/dying.htm

- Gott, Merryn. (2011). Living with Ageing and Dying: International Perspectives on End of Life Care for Older People. Section II

- Horsfall, Debbie & Yardley, Ainlsey & Leonard, Rosemary & Noonan, Kerrie & Rosenberg, John. (2015). End of Life at Home: Co-Creating an Ecology of Care. 10.13140/RG.2.1.3507.4008

- Horsfall, Debbie & Noonan, Kerrie & Leonard, Rosemary. (2013). Bringing our Dying Home: How caring for someone at end of life builds social capital and develops compassionate communities. Health Sociology Review. 21. 373-382. 10.5172/hesr.2012.21.4.373

- Niziolomski J, Rickson J, Marquez-Grant N, Pawlett M, 'Soil Science Related to the Human Body After Death', literature review produced for The Corpse Project March 2016

- Noonan, Kerrie & Horsfall, Debbie & Leonard, Rosemary & Rosenberg, John (2016). Developing death literacy. Progress in Palliative Care. 24. 160108221646007. 10.1080/09699260.2015.1103498

- NOUS Group 6 July 2018, Final Report 'Compassionate Communities Feasibility Study' Department of Health https://palliativecare.org.au/wp-content/uploads/dlm_uploads/2018/09/Compassionate-Communities-Final-Report-min.pdf

- Rashmi AS, Vangara Namratha, P Sahithi, 'Capsula Mundi: An Organic Burial Pod', Research Article European Journal of Advances in Engineering and Technology ISSN 2394-658x

- Rawlings, Deb & Litster, Caroline & Miller-Lewis, Lauren & Tieman, Jennifer & Swetenham, Kate. (2019). The voices of death doulas about their role in end-of-life care. Health & Social Care in the Community. 28. 10.1111/hsc.12833

- Small World Consulting, February 2016, Report for The Corpse Project: 'The Carbon Impacts of Choices with the Body After Death: Four Scenarios' http://www.thecorpseproject.net/wp-content/uploads/2016/06/Carbon-assessment-final-report-02-16.pdf

- Sources – 'Cemetery' Wikipedia

- Swerissen, Hal and Duckett, Stephen J 'What can we do to help Australians die the way they want to', Med J Aust 2015; 202 (1): 10-11. || doi: 10.5694/mja14.01580. Published online: 19 January 2015 https://www.mja.com.au/journal/2015/202/1/what-can-we-do-help-australians-die-way-they-want

- Van der Laan, Sandra & Moerman, Lee. (2017). It's your funeral: An investigation into death care and the funeral industry in Australia

- Venbrux, Eric. (2017). How the Tiwi Construct the Deceased's Postself in Mortuary Ritual. Anthropological Forum. 27. 1-14. 10.1080/00664677.2017.1287055

- www.Oldest.org – oldest cemeteries

- www.napoleon.org

- www.britannica.com – Cremation

NOTES

1   IBIS World Report 2019

2   IBIS World Report 2019

3   Ramsey Creek blog, Billy and Kimberley Campbell www.memorialecosystems.com 'Cemeteries, Ecological Restoration, Deep Time, and Net Present Value'

4   Clare Turnham, interview conducted at the NHFA Conference 2019

5   'Crestone – Gateway to the Higher Realms' by James McCalpin

6   Alison Wonderland, follow up discussions via email, Crestone Colorado USA 2019

7   Alison Wonderland, follow up discussions via email, Crestone Colorado USA 2019

8   Alison Wonderland, follow up discussions via email, Crestone Colorado USA 2019

9   The Australian Museum – 'Disposing of the Dead – Cremation' https://australianmuseum. net.au/about/history/exhibitions/death-the-last-taboo/disposing-of-the-dead-cremation/

10 'The Burning Question – how cremation became our last great act of self-determination', Thomas Laqueur - https://www.theguardian.com/books/2015/oct/30/burning-question-how-cremation-became-last-great-act-self-determination-thomas-laqueur

11 The Burning Question – how cremation became our last great act of self-determination', Thomas Laqueur

12 The Australian Museum – 'Disposing of the Dead – Cremation'

Right: Capuchin Monks in a Crypt in Brno, Czech Republic

CO JSME MY · BUDETE I VY

AUTHOR'S BIOGRAPHY

Bec is a mother of one and is originally from the Blue Mountains in NSW. She started her working career in Sydney before making the move to Tasmania in late 2006. Over her career she has worked in various industries including finance, real estate and the law but in 2011, she found her path into the funeral industry and stayed there until mid-2017 working across the many roles offered in the contemporary funeral industry; including pre planning, administration, mortuary, funeral arranging and directing. Retraining as an end of life doula and becoming an independent funeral director she has worked in home-based death care and family-led funerals ever since.

Bec has also been actively working to advance the mission of You n' Taboo which is the education and advocacy service she co-founded with her partner in 2016. In 2018 Bec was awarded a Churchill Fellowship to undertake international research and report on changes and disruptions in the end of life space which saw her travel through 6 countries exploring alternatives to contemporary ceremony and body disposal. A link to her report can be found by online at the Winston Churchill Memorial Trust.

Most recently Bec was selected as one of ten speakers to give a TEDx Presentation in Hobart, titled 'Three Steps into the Heart of Home Funeral'. In her spare time, she enjoys reading, writing, photography, camping and travel but what makes her most contented is time with her family. The subjects of death and dying, natural burial and the DIY approach to death care are her passion and she loves being out in the community raising awareness and promoting good honest conversations, she is a dedicated advocate for positive change.

Bec is the President of the Natural Death Advocacy Network (NDAN) in Australia and also the Australian Home Funeral Alliance (AHFA).

Email: bec@yountaboo.com
Website: www.yountaboo.com

www.ingramcontent.com/pod-product-compliance
Lightning Source LLC
Chambersburg PA
CBHW051558030426
42334CB00031B/3254